OTHER BOOKS BY THIS AUTHOR:

The Doctors Guide to Starting Your Practice/Career Right

The Doctors Guide to Eliminating Debt

The Doctors Guide to Real Estate Investing for Busy Professionals

The Doctors Guide to Navigating a Financial Crisis

THE
DOCTORS
GUIDE TO

Smart Career Alternatives and Retirement

DR. CORY S. FAWCETT

The Doctors Guide to Smart Career Alternatives and Retirement
By Dr. Cory S. Fawcett © 2017

Print ISBN: 978-1-61206-120-7
eBook ISBN: 978-1-61206-121-4

Interior and Cover Design by: Fusion Creative Works, FusionCW.com
Lead Editor: Jennifer Regner

For more information, visit FinancialSuccessMD.com.

To purchase this book at highly discounted prices, go to AlohaPublishing.com or email alohapublishing@gmail.com.

Published by

AlohaPublishing.com

Printed in the United States of America

Dedication

Name _____

Address _____

_____ Date _____

R̥x

This book is dedicated to my wife, Carolyn, and my boys, Brian and Keith, who traveled with me on this journey through the various phases of my career and stood beside me all along the way.

Signature _____ **Dr. Cory S. Fawcett** _____

Contents

I wrote this book to give you options to think about when your work is no longer satisfying. Let me help you to understand why you want to make a change, where your finish line is, and how to find joy in your work for the rest of your life.

A career change, including retirement, is a big step, and for many doctors it is also irreversible. Before you take that step, analyze your goals and your reasoning to determine whether you need a career change or retirement.

Doctors who have a plan for what they will retire to are more likely to make the move successfully. Those who don't, often are back at work within a year. Think about who you will be and what you will do in retirement, or even whether you want to completely stop practicing.

If you still enjoy practicing medicine but want a change, consider a different approach to your practice that allows you to change your work pace or reduce your stress. Enhance those parts of practicing medicine you enjoy, and eliminate or reduce those you don't.

Consider repurposing your skills, knowledge, and experience in a way that gives you joy. You have many skills to offer an employer beyond your degree. Explore nonclinical alternatives that engage your abilities and experience with a complete change of pace.

Chapter 10: Lifestyle Changes in Retirement

Your life has likely been very scheduled throughout your career. Be sure to make a schedule for your new life—make a list of the things you want to do and prioritize them, so you don't let the great stuff get covered over by the good stuff. Yes, your to-do list will still exist after you retire.

Chapter 11: Beyond the Finish Line and Estate Issues

You may have a significant inheritance to pass on to your family. You—or more accurately, your heirs—may even be faced with a significant estate tax if you don't do everything right. If you have a significant estate, you may include philanthropy in your plans. You can make some incredible gifts while you are still alive to see them work.

Introduction

According to the 2016 "Survey of America's Physicians: Practice Patterns and Perspectives," conducted by Merritt Hawkins on behalf of The Physicians Foundation, during the next three years, 14.4% of physicians will retire, 13.5% will switch to a nonclinical career, and 9.8% will cut back to part time. More than one-third of working physicians want a dramatic change in their career.

You may have thought, possibly many times if your current job has aspects you dislike, about how much you'd really like to retire. You may honestly feel you are ready to stop working altogether and vacation for the rest of your life. You've worked hard for many years, and you deserve to kick back and relax.

Or, perhaps you don't really want to *retire*—you simply want to *get away from those aspects of your job you don't like,* which could be too many working hours, not enough vacation, colleagues you don't respect, too much call, production quotas, etc. You may truly love practicing medicine, but hate the ancillary things that go along with it. Maybe you chose a position or specialty that doesn't meet your expectations and now you feel trapped.

Retirement is like a carrot hanging out in front of you. But is that carrot as tasty as you imagine? You save for it. You dream and plan for what you will do when you get there. You wish for that time to be *now*. But longing for tomorrow can sap the enjoyment out of today.

Tomorrow's hopes should not steal today's joy.

I wrote this book to give you options to think about when your work is no longer satisfying.

Can you absorb all the joy life has to offer today, if you spend your time wishing it was tomorrow and you were retired?

Don't get me wrong—I'm not opposed to retiring if it's the right choice for you. It is the obsession with retirement that can rob you of mindful focus on today. It is too easy to get stuck on this one issue and let it play over and over in your mind. With each new playing, you become a little more dissatisfied and confused, until you don't know what to do next.

INTRODUCTION

If you don't find joy in your work and you are persistently long-ing for the day when it is over, why not stop what you are doing now and move on to something you love? Don't wait until you are 65 to do what you love to do. Every day you spend doing a job you hate is 24 more hours of your life you gave up. Life is too short to waste any of it. And, if you want to quit practicing clinical medicine, retirement is not your only option.

A healthy balance is what you seek. Some planning for tomor-row is good, but don't overdo it; keep it in proper prospective. If job dissatisfaction is the reason you long for retirement, three chapters in this book offer suggestions to help you transition to something that will provide joy in your work. Not all doctors see patients for a living; a wide variety of alternatives can utilize your degree, expertise, and experience.

Let me help you find joy in your work each and every day. You may never retire—you might want to work right up until your death or disability and love every minute. You may, like me, want a change of pace after twenty years of hard work. You would still like to do your job but at a slower pace—one you can keep up for a few more years.

When you begin planning for your retirement, it is important to know how much you need to save so you don't run the risk of putting too much money away for the future and not leaving enough to enjoy today. Remember Dickens's character Ebenezer

Scrooge in *A Christmas Story*? He was so obsessed with saving his money for later, he never used any of it to enjoy his life. You don't want to be like him. There is no need to pile everything into your savings at the expense of enjoying life today.

Determine how much is enough and save toward that goal, then put the rest of your money to better use. I call this establishing a *finish line*. Without a finish line, you not only run the risk of becoming a hoarder like Scrooge, you also risk staying on the treadmill long after you should have gotten off to walk. You will miss many of the joys in life if you increase your stockpile of money beyond your needs.

Do you have a finish line—that total amount of money you need to save to secure your financial future? If not, how will you know when you have saved enough? Because once you have saved enough, you can divert the money you were putting into savings for other uses that bring joy to your life.

Without a finish line, you can become a money hoarder. Hoarders are never happy, since they never have enough. You will have enough.

On the other extreme, without a finish line—no goal to shoot for, no plan for the future—you may be haphazardly spending your money, and you might be sorry when you are older and have nothing to fall back on.

If you don't know where you are going, you will never know when you get there.

Come with me on this journey to understand why you want to make a change, where your finish line is, and how to find joy in your work for the rest of your life—and rest easy knowing you've planned adequately for your retirement. You work hard and deserve to enjoy some great rewards and to have a happy journey along the way. If it turns out retirement is the right answer for you, then I will show you how to make that move smoothly and at a time of your choosing.

Life is a journey. Make it a good one!

Chapter 1

KNOW WHY YOU WANT A CHANGE

A career change is a big step, and for many doctors it is also irreversible.

Once you give up privileges, malpractice insurance, and your license, you may never be able to go back. A long pause in your practice will create doubt that you still have the knowledge and skills needed to do the job, if you try to return. A partner or employer may require remedial education to assure them you can still perform. With that in mind, it is crucial that you are absolutely certain of this move. Analyze your goals and your reasoning to be sure a career change or retirement is the right answer for you.

Burning bridges is always a frightening proposition. This is part of why retirement/career change is a very difficult decision for a doctor to make. Maybe what you really need to do is cut back on your hours or make some changes in your current practice environment, rather than commit to leaving your practice. Let's take a closer look at the usual reasons for wanting to retire, to help you pinpoint the motives driving your decision.

LOOKING FOR SOMETHING NEW

YOU WANT TO TRAVEL BEFORE YOU GET TOO OLD

This is a good one, but it presumes you cannot travel while you still work. Do not postpone your travel "bucket list" until after retirement, as your health may not allow it by then and you may miss out entirely. During our recent Mediterranean cruise, my wife and I noticed we were one of the youngest couples on the boat, and many of the other travelers did not get around very well. It would be good to do your traveling while you are still young enough to be mobile.

Make good use of your vacation time throughout your career. Never let vacation days expire. Some doctors use the phrase "I never use all my vacation time" as if it were a medal of honor, when in reality it is a poorly thought-out decision. Most of us work long and arduous hours and the need for vacation time should not be underestimated.

Depending on your situation, vacation allotments may vary widely. Some doctors have greater control over their schedule and can take any amount of vacation they desire. The extra time off will only result in a lower income. I worked in such a situation and took nine to twelve weeks of vacation annually during my career. That is one of the benefits of being in private practice. You may have vacation and continuing medical education (CME) time more restricted by an employer and might be limited to four to six weeks a year.

The key is to use the time you have wisely. For example, add three vacation/CME days to a weekend you already have off. This creates a five-day weekend. If you have six weeks off allotted for the year—30 working days—this method will give you ten five-day vacations throughout the year. This may effectively convert your six weeks off into ten weeks of travel. This becomes even more effective if you have one day a week out of the office to tack on as well. For example, if you have Tuesday off during the week and were to take three days of vacation on Wednesday through Friday, you effectively converted three days of vacation into a six-day trip. Flying out Monday evening after work adds on even more time to the trip. You can also use CME conferences for travel to a city you want to explore and, either before or after the meeting, add some vacation days to the trip. This has the added benefit of making a vacation partially tax deductible.

There are ways to get more time off if that is what you desire. If you are in private practice, taking extra time off will simply result in a lower income. If you are employed, you may be able to negotiate for more time off; if needed, you can lower your salary to accommodate this. Of course, this is more easily done during your initial contract negotiations for your employment. At that time, you have the most power at the negotiating table because they want you to join them. Afterward, once you are in their employ, your negotiating power is much less and you might actually need to change jobs to obtain more time off.

If you are financially ready to retire, the lower income from taking extra time off will not be an issue, especially since continuing to work generates more income than being retired would. If you are not financially ready to retire, consider scaling back your spending to accommodate your desire to travel. The big house may have lost its importance to you, when your kids are gone and you want to travel.

One friend of mine had a clever concept he used during his career. He decided early on to move his retirement target date out an extra two years. This gave him an additional 104 weeks of income production during his working years. He then spread that over his career by taking an extra three weeks of vacation each year. He was able to use that extra time with his family when his children were young, instead of having more years in retirement. He and his family were very happy with that decision, and his lifetime income and number of working days were not decreased as a result. This had an added bonus of allowing his retirement account two more years of growth as well. Think outside the box and you will come up with some great ideas.

YOU SEEK A DIFFERENT MISSION NOW

Some of you may have discovered a calling to do something like practice medicine in a developing country. Or maybe you have always wanted to do this but couldn't because of financial constraints. Later in your career, when your financial situation has improved, you are ready to scratch this itch. Maybe your parents need you to help them as they age. There could be some aspect of your practice that you always wanted to do but were reluctant to pursue, maybe because it didn't pay well. Pursuing this avenue could mean finding greater fulfillment in your career. Having something on the "back burner" you always wanted to do can be a burr under your saddle until you finally take the step to do it.

AFTER 30 YEARS, YOU ARE READY FOR A CHANGE

Sometimes you're simply ready to do something different with your life. Some specialties treat very few diagnoses. After years of this, you can become bored by seeing the same old thing. This is often labeled a "midlife crisis." Take careful stock of what it is that you don't like about your current situation before pulling the trigger on a change. And if there truly is nothing you can fix to make it better, maybe it is time to move on.

Sometimes, though, you don't need to change your job to find this new excitement. Taking a class at the local college to study something new or trying a new hobby may be enough to renew the spark in your life. Pick up some new activities to do with your spouse or friends. There are many ways to spice up your life besides retirement. Be sure it is really the job change you need and not something else before taking the leap.

YOU'RE READY TO FOLLOW ANOTHER DREAM

You may have dreams of working in a field other than healthcare. Many of those dreams got put off while you pursued your doctoring career. I recorded a music album while in medical school and soon realized I must make a choice. Music, like medicine, would require a full-time commitment in order to make a living, so I couldn't do both. I decided on the sure thing and played music as a hobby. I was a worship leader in church, had a men's quartet, and performed at various one-night events, always thinking I would pick up music on a larger scale again when I retired from medicine. In reality, I continued to play music all along the way, just not full time.

If you have another dream, deciding when you can go for it is key. It would be sad to go to your grave wondering what could have been if you had pursued your dream. Don't die with regrets. You also don't have to live the dream in its entirety to fulfill it. For example, being part of a men's quartet that performs monthly versus going on a world tour. Either may suffice, yet they have very different career implications and requirements.

YOU DON'T LIKE YOUR WORK

This is a tough issue. Is it really being a doctor you don't like, or is there something about your job that needs changing? Perhaps you did pick the wrong profession. If that is your situation, don't waste another day of your shorter-than-you-realize life doing something you don't like. Look into something else and start the process of changing professions now.

I will talk later in the book of other things you can do with a valuable doctorate. The MD, DO, DDS, or any other doctorate initials behind your name carry value in many industries.

If, on the other hand, you like what you do but other things about the job are getting to you, take the time to analyze what it is you dislike, then make the necessary changes. Stop doing the parts you don't like. Drop procedures you don't like. Get rid of problem patients. Do whatever it takes to make your job fulfilling again.

As a general surgeon, my problem areas were thoracic and vascular surgery. I did not enjoy those cases. I only did them because they paid well and I was worried my income would suffer if I didn't continue to do them. Only after I became debt-free did I finally have the courage to eliminate them, and I enjoyed my practice so much more. If your job does not allow you to control the areas you want to change, then it may be time to move on to one that better fits your needs.

IT'S NO FUN ANYMORE

TAKING CALL IS TAKING ITS TOLL

As you age, taking call can become a big factor if you work in a specialty with lots of emergencies. I have noticed over the years that I don't recover from being up all night like I used to. As a resident, I could work 36 straight hours, then get a good night's sleep and be back in business. Now it takes several days to recover from working all night. Everyone will be affected by this differently, but quitting is not the only solution.

I know of one female doctor, whose husband was also a doctor, who quit because she felt taking call was ruining her home life. It created too much work for the day after call, and she couldn't get home at a decent hour to be with her family. She never considered lightening or emptying her schedule the day after call to leave room for the emergencies she would pick up. She was worried about losing income if she put some space in her schedule, but with a second high-income earner in the family, income shouldn't have been an issue. Having her post-call days lighter may have given her the breathing room she needed to maintain the work-life balance she was seeking.

My weekend call was three days, Friday through Sunday. By Monday morning, I was tired and usually had a lot of add-on work to do. I learned early on that leaving Monday's schedule open after a call weekend, with no appointments or surgeries, improved my life by leaps and bounds. I had plenty of work to do that day without trying to work around an already fully scheduled day. It was also helpful for my office staff and patients, who did not have to reschedule to accommodate a big surgery I needed to do on short notice.

Initially, I worried about losing income by not booking any patients that day, but I usually ended up doing a full day's work that day anyway and since there was room in the schedule to make the additions, I was less stressed about getting it all done. And I no longer dreaded the Monday after a call weekend. Think about adjustments you can engineer to make taking call more palatable.

There are many ways to improve taking call without the need to drop it altogether. I already mentioned not scheduling a full day after call. But another thing to consider is how you prioritize the calls. Many doctors feel they need to drop everything when the beeper calls. That is seldom the case. Unless someone will die without your immediate attention, you can finish what you are doing first. No hip needs to be fixed at midnight. Fix it in the daylight when both you and your crew will be rested. The emergency physician can start your diabetic patient on the right treatment at 3:00 a.m. and you can see them at 7:00 a.m. to see how the treatment is working. You do not need to go see them at 3:00 a.m., in addition to the emergency physician. Admissions that happen in the middle of your clinic time can almost always be attended to after your office patients are seen and do not require you to reschedule all those patients. These are small things that make a big difference in your day and the level of frustration created by the unexpected. So many doctors ruin their lives by not attributing the correct amount of urgency to the issues that arise during the day.

Even if you are an employed physician within a hospital, university, or large group practice, you can't have the attitude of "My boss would never let me lighten the day post-call . . ." You may be surprised and may also find that making such schedule changes are worth it to the organization in order to maintain your health and a good flow of patients in the office. Rescheduling patients is a huge burden on your staff and your patients. If you present it right, it is a good thing for your organization as well as for you. Rescheduled patients are unhappy—they made special arrangements to be there and an appointment change with one hour's notice may be an imposition for them. Organizations are seeking happy patients, and a light post-call day makes happy patients, staff, and doctors. Also, finding another doctor to take on your job if you were to leave is a big deal, so you may discover your employer is willing to work with you to find ways to retain you for the long haul. If not, then consider moving on since you are not in a healthy environment for doctors.

THE BIG CASES ARE WEARING ON YOU

As you age, the tougher cases get exponentially tougher. For surgeons, standing for long periods of time at the operating table gets harder. Some surgeons have limited the kinds of cases they will take by the length of time they can last between bathroom breaks. Non-surgeons may not have the stamina to see a full day of patients anymore, especially at the pace required by a quota. Maybe you could practice several more years if you decreased the number of patients you see per day.

Keeping experienced doctors in the game longer will help decrease the physician shortage we are facing for the next few decades. It is ironic that often the bigger cases/tougher problems require the greater expertise of an experienced doctor, yet it is the experienced doctor who wants to limit those cases due to the fatigue factor.

If this sounds like you, assess whether cutting back, finding more flexible working conditions, retirement, or changing professions is the right answer to moving at a slower pace.

PRESSURE AND STRESS ARE BUILDING

Everyone handles pressure differently. Some can take a lot of pressure and not notice much stress. Others are incapacitated by just a little. This is one of the factors people use in picking a specialty. Those who don't do well under pressure should not go into emergency medicine, for example.

There are several types of pressure you may encounter. Participation in a malpractice case is not only very stressful but also drags on for several years. The risk of such a case is a heavy burden for some doctors. Death is an issue all doctors face, but some specialties, like oncology, face it more frequently than a pediatrician might. How you handle death—especially the unexpected death, which is very stressful—can change over time. Production quotas and financial issues create a performance stress that can be hard to deal with.

You may have chosen a specialty beyond your pressure tolerance. Or, you may have reached your lifetime limit. Twenty-five years in the emergency department takes a toll. The stigma involved in seeking help for this issue causes many doctors to keep suppressing it instead of addressing it. Is it possible for you to make adjustments to lessen the pressure you experience, such as switching from the emergency department of a busy hospital to an urgent care facility? If not, then retirement or a change of profession is in order before you burn out or develop PTSD, depression, or suicidal ideations.

Sometimes it is your spouse, family, or colleagues who will notice you are too stressed out before you do. Be open to others sharing their concerns with you. Make the changes you need to make to avoid negative stress-induced consequences.

FEAR OF MALPRACTICE SUITS

I hear this a lot from older doctors who haven't had a big malpractice case haunt them. They want to get out of medicine before it happens. Others talk about cutting out the risky cases to cut down on the chance of a malpractice suit.

If you are working with the worry of malpractice all the time, you will not be at your best. I remember once assisting on an emergency caesarean section with a rapidly deteriorating baby. The obstetrician was visibly flustered and stated as we handed off the child to a team who began CPR, "I am responsible for that child until he's 21." This was not only a worry over the malpractice issue—since that child, if he had any problems related to the birth, could sue her up until he was an adult— but also it was about the heavy burden all doctors bear for the outcomes of their patients. Some bear this better than others.

Many doctors have those moments when they wonder if they could have done better, been faster, or come up with a better solution. Those outside the profession don't realize the weight this burden puts on you. Was that bad outcome your fault, or was there no way to prevent it? It's OK if these feelings are only occasional. It's not OK if they haunt you daily. If this fear is controlling your work life, a change may be in order.

DREADING THE NEXT BOARD EXAM

Board certification has become a hot issue, and maintenance of certification even hotter. Initially, general surgeons had no certifying body. Then, we were certified once for life. Then, we were certified for ten years and needed to renew by taking another written exam. Now, it is a three-year maintenance of certification. The timeline is getting ridiculously short. The main recertifying exam is difficult and requires a lot of study, on top of an already busy schedule.

Many doctors narrow their practices to only a few diagnoses, but the recertification exam covers everything in their field. Studying to pass a test covering topics you don't deal with anymore is difficult to justify. These exams are expensive in cost as well as the time investment needed to study, take prep courses, and sit for the exam.

Many doctors have told me, "That was my last board exam." You may be one of them. I am one of them. I've never had a problem passing my boards, but it takes a lot of extra effort to be sure I'm ready for the test. I feel your pain.

Some places will let you practice without current board certification, so that may be an option. But increasingly, credentialing in most practice settings requires you to be board certified/eligible to work. You might consider dropping one of your certifications if you are boarded in multiple specialties, to lessen the impact. If you feel recertifying is too much at this point in your life and you will not be able to practice if you are not board-certified, it may be time to take down your shingle.

LOSING CONFIDENCE

If you are thinking your performance is not up to standard, you are right. Often, those around you will not speak up if you are slipping in your skills, as they may be afraid of your response to their suggestion. That is an awkward conversation most people would like to avoid. It would be better for you to stop practicing than to be forced out for incompetence or cause a major problem because of a mistake. Leave on your terms and at the top of your game.

It is possible you will not perceive this decline in your performance. If someone is hinting at this, take the hint. If you have a major health issue, consider retiring from active practice. You might be able to recover from a major stroke, but others may always wonder if you still have all your faculties. Don't take the chance. Follow the age-old advice of Hippocrates to "first, do no harm."

TOO OLD

This is a hard one. No one wants to be told they are too old to do the job anymore. But the reality is, it is sometimes true. Articles are being published about a mandatory retirement age for physicians. There are strong and heated arguments for both sides of the issue. Age is not really the issue, but competence is what is at stake.

If you think you are too old, you are. If someone is saying you are too old, you are. Don't wait until you are asked to quit by some overseeing body. Bow out on your own and with a good reputation. Let your patients, colleagues, and staff remember you at your best.

FRUSTRATIONS OF HEALTHCARE REFORM

ELECTRONIC HEALTH RECORDS (EHR)

The dislike of using electronic health records is almost a universal feeling among older doctors. The younger ones grew up using the EHR and know of no other way. Older doctors are often unhappy with this change. No one likes change, especially if it is forced upon them. EHRs are here to stay, so all doctors need to step up to the plate. The programs will become more user-friendly and continue to improve with time, but they will not go away.

Many doctors gripe about this constantly. They walk into the room complaining, sit down at the computer complaining, work on the computer complaining, and get up to leave the room complaining. One even told me he counted how many problems he experienced with the EHR program during the day and stopped counting at 150. I can't help but think how this amount of complaining is affecting his attitude towards work, his relationship with his patients, and his personal well-being.

Are you complaining about, tolerating, or embracing your EHR? If this is your reason for wanting to retire, please reevaluate it. A simple attitude adjustment may be in order. I understand the sentiment, since I was once one of the complainers. Changing my attitude fixed the problem.

I attended an EHR training session one day and griped to the instructor for five minutes about things she couldn't change. Eventually she said, "Well I can see how this day is going to go." It was like getting hit in the face with a two-by-four. She was only there to teach me how it worked, and she had no control over the things I didn't like. I was spewing my anger about the EHR on her—but my anger should not have existed. Don't let a computer program ruin your day, like I was letting it ruin mine and consequently hers—especially since neither of us could control or change the necessity to deal with it and make it work.

Many doctors have found that using a scribe to document the patient visit has enabled them to be more present with their patients and still meet all the EHR documentation requirements. If you do not already have this assistance, maybe the addition of a scribe will help you to keep up your work flow with less stress regarding the computer. Of course, you are still responsible for the charting and need to review what the scribe has typed and then sign off on your patient visit notes that the scribe has created. Working with a scribe takes some adjustment, but ultimately can be an efficient solution as the cost of a scribe is far lower than the production value of a doctor. If you hire a scribe and can see several more patients a day because of it, you and your employer will be money ahead. You will also make gains in your mental well-being.

You are an intelligent person or you would not have made it this far. You can figure out how to use the EHR so it doesn't ruin your life. Don't let a computer program drive you out of medicine. Completing medical records is not why you went through all those years of training. Keep it in perspective. You can improve your ability to use the program by taking classes, studying the manual, asking your employer to bring in a physician expert on the program to work with you, and learning from the others on your team how they do it, especially the younger ones.

Rather than just griping about it, take an active role and constructively voice your concerns so you will help formulate the changes and improvements in the future programing. Get some help and make it work.

DECLINING REIMBURSEMENT WITH INCREASING HASSLE

It is hard to keep doing your job if you get paid less every year. Other industries get a raise as time goes by. The medical profession, for the most part, has been taking pay cuts. Some of the cuts are not in actual salary, but in requiring you to do more to earn the same salary.

One doctor told me, "Each new rule adds thirty minutes of work to my day, without an income increase to compensate for it." Another said, "After a full day of patients in the office, it takes me almost another full day to complete all the required charting."

If this is your concern, you may do better in a nonclinical field of work. Sometimes you simply want to get paid for *all* the hours you work.

THE HOSPITAL IS PUSHING YOU OUT OR TRYING TO BUY YOU OUT

Over the last decade, the number of doctors becoming employees has been increasing. Hospitals are buying up doctors' practices at an alarming rate. If you have been in private practice for 30 years, you may not want to become someone's employee, but holding out may not be financially possible. This may be the tipping point to push you into retirement. However, if you are not ready to retire for any other reason, rethink being bought out. It might not be as bad as you think.

I left my private practice after twenty years and was bought out by my partners, not a hospital. I then started doing locum tenens work and eventually went to work part time as an employee of another hospital system, and it made a nice transition for me. I was going to have to sell out eventually, so why not then? I could then work part time, on my terms, and when I was finally ready to quit practicing medicine altogether, I could just walk away without the need to find a buyer. In fact, that is exactly what I did in February 2017, when I stopped practicing clinical medicine altogether and focused on teaching doctors to live a better life and improve their financial situation.

I did not want to give up my private practice and become an employee, but after weighing the pros and cons for my situation, it seemed like a good move for me at the time. Working part time in my private practice was not possible under our partnership contract, so a change of some sort was needed. That change turned into an incredible opportunity for me.

I have worked in both a private practice model and an employment model. In my book *The Doctors Guide to Starting Your Practice Right* and in my blog at DrCorySFawcett.com, I have listed the pros and cons of employment and private practice. Look those over and determine for yourself which model fits you best. If the model that seems a better fit is not where you are at the moment, maybe a change will be a good thing for you.

UNDERSTAND YOUR REASONS

Understanding the reason behind your desire to retire or change careers is important. I just covered several, but maybe you have a different reason. Come up with a clear reason for why you want to make a change, or you may regret the decision. If there is an issue you need to deal with, you will be sorry if you choose to quit instead of confronting that issue. Even if you retire, the problem may not go away until you deal with it. Implement a solution and confirm you still want to make a change after it is resolved.

This would be a good time to seek the guidance of a career transition coach or a preretirement financial planner before burning any bridges. There are many such coaches available. Getting a clear picture of your options can be an invaluable step.

BE SURE RETIRING IS WHAT YOU NEED

There was a time in my life when I was very unhappy with practicing medicine, and I was thinking about quitting. My church was actually looking for a full-time worship leader at the time, but taking that position would have meant a big lifestyle change for my family. My wife and I were teaching a Crown Financial Ministries course, and I brought this up to the group during prayer requests. One of the students asked me to consider if I was being called to retire, or if I was just having a bad day.

I hadn't thought about that. Was I being called to retire? That Sunday night I asked the group to pray for me to help me discover the answer to that question.

The next week was one of the best weeks I ever had in medicine. On Monday, the emergency department (ED) called me, even though I wasn't on call, asking me to help with a patient who needed a procedure only I could do. Could I please help? I came in to see the patient, and the ED doctor thanked me and told me he was so glad I was available. The next day I was walking past the recovery room when a code blue was called. I happened to be right there, and I saved the patient's life. It had been a long time since I could directly point to an event and say I saved a life.

Several of my patients that week thanked me and told me they were so glad I was there to help them. I had not heard a thank you in the office for quite some time.

Many more little things happened, and by the end of the week I was getting a clear message that I was not being called to retire. So, something else must be making me unhappy. During class the next Sunday, I related the events of the week and concluded I should continue practicing medicine. One of the students suggested that maybe all I needed was a sabbatical to clear my mind.

That seemed like a good idea. The next day, after seeing an opening in my schedule, I asked the office manager to book me out for the whole month of May for a short sabbatical.

During the sabbatical, I set out to accomplish two tasks: read the New Testament, which I had not done for a few years, and figure out what was bothering me. During the first day of reading, it hit me. A big neon sign jumped from a page in my Bible, or so it seemed to me. Right there, plain as day, was my problem: bitterness.

I was bitter over a disagreement that took place at the hospital the year before. Every time I drove by the hospital or saw a patient, I felt it. Every surgery reminded me of the anger. My life was being ruined by my bitterness toward someone else. **It was like I was drinking poison and hoping my enemy would die.**

I changed gears and did a quick Bible study on bitterness, and within a few days I had found the solution. I needed to forgive the person who wronged me. My problem, the thing that was driving me to consider quitting medicine, was my anger toward someone at the hospital.

I decided to forgive. In order for the forgiveness to feel real, I also did something special to make amends. I made a large donation to the hospital to make it clear to myself the bitterness was gone.

Just a few days into the sabbatical, I was done with my quest. My feelings of wanting to quit were gone, and I was able to enjoy the rest of the month in peace. I came back to work in June with a new lease on life, ready to be a doctor again.

If I had quit medicine over an anger issue, I would have been sorry. I would have thrown away a career for the wrong reasons, and the anger issue would still have been there.

Find out what is really driving your decision and address it. If there is no underlying problem to address and you still want to retire, then you will know you are making the decision for the right reasons. Don't make an irreversible mistake like I almost made. If you don't address the real problem, you will just carry it into your retirement and be just as unhappy there. If the problem is inside you—such as enabling people, being too demanding, or not speaking up for what you need—this will follow you right into retirement and continue to impact every relationship there as well. Be sure you understand the problem and solve it. Don't use retirement to run away from something or you will be sorry.

In my case, my religious convictions played a big part in solving my dissatisfaction issue. You may not have this option in your life, but if you are considering leaving medicine, please seek some outside guidance before you pull the trigger. You will undoubtedly grow in the process.

Here are a few additional questions to ask yourself to be sure you are addressing the real problem:

- Am I bored?

- Am I worn out?

- Am I depressed?

- Am I having a problem with a partner or coworker?

- Am I angry about something?

- Do I want to live in a different part of the country?

- Will this change be more fulfilling?

- Do I need a sabbatical?

- Is a recent bad outcome dragging me down?

- What do I expect to gain by retiring or changing careers?

- Is my desire coming from within me or from somewhere outside?

- Is the real reason hiding behind the reason I am claiming?

Be absolutely certain of your desire before you make the move. Whether you decide to retire, cut back, or move to another profession, be sure you do it with a clear understanding that you are making the right choice, at the right time, to improve your future well-being.

Chapter 2

WHAT WILL YOU DO
IF YOU RETIRE?

Retiring at the age of 50 had been my goal since I was in medical school. I don't know where the number came from, but it was there from the start. As I neared my target date, because of my long-term planning, I was financially ready to retire. I had enough tax-advantaged savings and enough passive income to support my family comfortably.

I told one of my partners I was planning to retire and he asked me what I was planning to retire to. The question caught me by surprise, as I had never thought about that. He told me about all the doctors he had watched retire. Those who had a plan were able to make the move successfully. They had something they were going to do with their free time. They had a purpose. Those who didn't have a plan were often back to work within a year.

Three things tend to drive recently retired doctors back to work: boredom, lack of funds, and a loss of identity or purpose.

I thought about that a lot over the next few days. I didn't have a plan. I was locked in on the age to retire and had not formulated a plan for my postretirement years. I figured I would have plenty of time on my hands after I stopped working and would formulate a plan then. By the end of the week, I had decided not to retire yet. First, I would work on a plan.

I had a lot of ideas. I even started doing things differently as I worked. I cut back my hours a bit during this period as I played with different ideas for my future. I started a radio talk show on medicine, which was a lot of fun. I began a weekly medical clinic at the Gospel Rescue Mission. I began playing more music, wrote some jingles, and toyed with the notion of getting back into songwriting.

It became very clear to me during this period of reflection that I was at great risk of becoming one of those doctors who retired and then a short time later went back to work. I was so grateful to have heard my partner's council about formulating a plan first. Of the reasons for returning to work listed above, I had the funds issue covered, but the identity/purpose and boredom issues would likely push me back to work in short order if I didn't develop a good plan to occupy my time, energy, and talent.

REPURPOSING MY CAREER

During this time, a former general surgery resident, who had trained his entire fourth year with my group in our rural residency program, contacted us looking for some help. He lived in a small town with only three general surgeons. The prior December, his two partners both left. He was suddenly alone and burning out, taking call 24/7. He had a new partner coming in the fall and he wondered if someone in our group could cover for one week a month to help him make it until his new partner arrived. He was not satisfied with the random, rotating locum tenens surgeons the hospital hired and wanted someone he knew he could trust to cover his practice.

Since I was experimenting with new things at the time, both my kids were away at college, and my wife did not work outside our home and was able to travel with me, it seemed like a nice opportunity to try something new. After getting hospital privileges and a license in his state, I became an employee of one of my former residents for one week each month. I loved working in this new environment, a 25-bed critical access hospital (CAH). The people I encountered were so appreciative; several thanked me for coming. The work pace was so much slower than I was used to that it felt like I was on vacation, yet I was still actively using the skills I had honed over twenty years of practice.

That experience was so great, I felt it was my calling. This is what I could "retire to." I made the decision to leave my practice and work part time, providing call relief for surgeons nearby who worked alone in critical access hospitals. They needed some time off the beeper to keep them healthy and get a break, while I needed a change of pace—a win-win deal. I have devoted an entire chapter in this book to describing this fun and fulfilling work option. I decided a change in terminology was in order: I was no longer retiring, I was *repurposing*.

WHO WILL YOU BE IN RETIREMENT?

Make sure you have a viable plan formulated before you take the plunge into retirement. You will be excited for the move and having a plan will relieve some of your apprehension about the unknown. If you face an identity crisis, you will have a solution.

After you retire, how will you answer the question about what you do? Almost every time we meet someone new, the question of "What do you do?" comes up. Will you say you used to be a dentist, or whatever your profession was, or will you tell them about your new profession, avocation, or endeavor?

WHAT WILL YOU DO IF YOU RETIRE?

If you quit without a plan, will you feel you are less of a person? Will you feel you are not contributing to society? Will you feel like a drain or a failure?

Many people live into their 80s. If you were to retire at age 60 in good health, you might have 20 years of good productive life ahead of you. People have been paying you, as a doctor, for your knowledge, problem-solving skills, and experiences. Even after you retire, you will still have those valuable resources. There will still be many productive ways to use your mind with all the incredible experiences it holds. You can find other ways to use it that will make you feel fulfilled, bring you enjoyment, and give you a purpose.

You can have a second career using your knowledge, experience, and wisdom for other purposes. There are many famous examples of people who finished one career and then started another. This list of examples appeared in my book *The Doctors Guide to Eliminating Debt* and is worth repeating here.

Colonel Sanders developed the Kentucky Fried Chicken concept at age 65.

Laura Ingalls Wilder began writing the *Little House on the Prairie* series when she was 65.

Grandma Moses didn't begin painting until she was in her 80s.

Edmond Hoyle didn't write about card games until around age 70.

Ronald Reagan was elected to his first public office at age 55 and was 69 when he became president of the United States.

Former president Jimmy Carter started The Carter Center, which led to a Nobel Peace Prize, after leaving a career in politics at age 50.

Dr. Ben Carson retired from neurosurgery and ran for president of the United States at age 64.

QUIT WITH A PURPOSE

Everyone needs to have a purpose. Retirement without a plan for what to do with your time will leave you without a purpose. You will be unfulfilled.

Doctors tend to have very driven personalities and need to be always on the go. If your busy schedule comes to a sudden stop, you may not know what to do with yourself. The lack of a purpose may create a deafening silence. You need to be prepared for what you will be next, when you leave the practice of medicine. Or . . . don't leave it, just change it.

As I described earlier, if you enjoy being a doctor but want a different pace or a new specialty, you have many options. The world needs doctors, and the demand is not going to decrease anytime soon. Start reaching out for alternatives that can satisfy an unfulfilled dream or expectation. In later chapters, I will list some clinical and nonclinical alternatives to your typical practice.

I know one dentist who took up woodworking after he retired and found fulfillment making items for friends and relatives. What hobbies do you love that could be expanded when you are no longer working for a living? Imagine adding the experience you've gained and the bankroll you now have to your hobby. Combine that with the same passion you have put into your profession all these years. What can you do now that you would not have been able to do when you were 25?

IF YOU DON'T KNOW WHAT YOU WANT

Some of you will get lucky like I did and have an opportunity fall into your lap that allows you to try an alternative at the right time—when you are seeking alternatives. If you aren't sure what would make you happy, consider exploring your interests and talents to find a new direction. If you want some guidance, consider finding a life coach or career coach. For those more interested in self-exploration, you might try the books *StrengthsFinder 2.0* by Tom Rath (Gallup Press) or *Now, Discover Your Strengths* by Donald Clifton and Marcus Buckingham (Gallup Press). These avenues may uncover an area you would like to explore that you hadn't ever thought about.

The knowledge and experience you have acquired over your years as a doctor are valuable, and you can leverage that in a wide variety of hobbies and alternative professions. Practicing medicine is demanding work; if you enjoy using the expertise you've developed but want a lifestyle that's not dominated by the demands of your current practice or the board certification requirements, then use the options I list in the chapter titled Nonclinical Career Alternatives as a starting point for your exploration to discover what you'd like to do next.

You will be ahead of the game if you stop to think and determine what it is you are about to do: quit, leave, transition, or retire. Quitting what you are doing has the feel of "I'm out of here and never want to see this beeper again." It is a negative emotional move. Leaving feels more like you have now finished that phase of your life and it's time to move on. Transitioning is more like you have found a new calling and need to make a change to fulfill it. And retiring can be a mix of any of the previous ideas as well as stating you have reached the end of your productive years and are ready to relax and enjoy your grandchildren. Understanding the motivating factors will help make your next move successful.

You have great resources, a large palette of skills, and an almost unlimited canvas on which to paint your future. What will it look like? Who will you help? What can you create? The sky is the limit. Figure out what you want and go forth with a plan. Don't just quit—step out with a purpose and you will have a very fulfilling future. And once you have a plan, you can calculate your future financial needs for its achievement.

Chapter 3

CLINICAL CAREER ALTERNATIVES

If you desire some sort of change in your practice yet have decided not to get out of medicine completely, you can change your work pace or reduce your stress and continue to practice medicine in a variety of ways. Some alternatives involve continuing to see patients, but in a different capacity than in the past. Let's examine a few options that offer a change of pace.

WORKING PART TIME

The "Survey of America's Physicians: Practice Patterns and Perspectives," conducted by Merritt Hawkins on behalf of The Physicians Foundation, in 2016 found that 9.8% of the physicians they surveyed were planning to go part time within the next three years.

If you are one of those physicians, making this move will require the other doctors you are working with to buy into your idea. They may not want you to work part time, if their work-load or call burden increases as a result. They may want you to continue to pay your share of the overhead costs, if you are in private practice, even if you are using fewer services.

On the other hand, they may not want you to leave if you are willing to contribute to the call schedule and are available to help cover for them. They won't have to spend time or money recruiting if you stay and continue to contribute. Hospitals and private practices alike are having a hard time filling posi-tions in our current doctor shortage environment, so they will be motivated to work something out that will keep you in the group. The potential of being short one doctor for several years while they seek out your replacement might give you a strong position in the negotiations.

You will need to reach an agreement with your colleagues before moving ahead with any changes. Your current arrange-ment may not have a viable option for practicing part time. If you are in private practice, you may have a provision in your contract for splitting overhead equally, which will not play out well as you move to part time. As your work hours decrease, you will approach a point where you only bring in enough money to cover overhead and essentially are working for free. You might think that in private practice, with its greater flex-ibility over the employment model, working part time would be easier to accomplish, but that is not always the case. It is often easier to make a part-time arrangement as an employee.

In that model, you are working for a certain pay to see a certain number of patients. If you decrease the number of patients, there should be an equitable decrease in pay that would work for the situation.

Whether you are employed or are in private practice, there are many other ways to work part time. You may be able to job share with another doctor who wishes to also work part time. The two of you combined would make up one doctor and collect one doctor's worth of income. You can do shift work and limit the shifts you are responsible for, such as becoming a hospitalist or working at an urgent care facility. If you already work shifts, contract for fewer shifts. You can negotiate your contract for fewer hours, less call, and lower pay. Move to a market with a slower pace and fewer patients. Be open to all the options and find something that will work for you, and you can extend your career by cutting back to a workload that suits your current desires. The longer you extend your career, even working part time, the less impact you will have on the current physician shortage.

Never take the position of "I'm just an employee and this won't work for me." If you need a change in your working environment for whatever reason, work to make it happen. You will not know what your employer is willing to do until you have the conversation with them. Don't miss out on an opportunity simply because you didn't ask.

LOCUM TENENS

Locum tenens work is on the rise. In 2016, 11.5% of doctors were planning on doing locum tenens work in the near future, up from 9.1% in 2014, according to the Physicians Foundation surveys. Working as a locum tenens doctor has some tremendous benefits when it comes to working part time. As I've mentioned, I explored this option during my last year of full-time practice, when one of my former residents needed some help covering call. I was able to take one week per month off in my regular practice, which I usually used for vacation, and go work for him in a small town where the workload of covering the emergency department was much, much lower. It still felt like a vacation. This was my first experience with the concept of locum tenens work, and I found it very rewarding.

Do you have some preconceived notions about locum tenens work? Many doctors do. There are some stereotypes associated with this type of practice: only people who can't get or keep a job do locums, it's only good when you are starting and don't know what you want to do, all the good doctors have *real* jobs, etc. As with all stereotypes, they are not universally true or accurate. A seasoned doctor who becomes available to do locum tenens work will be in high demand.

Locum tenens work can be just about anything you want it to be. Drawing from general surgery as an example, you could choose from the following:

- ✓ Emergency department coverage only
- ✓ With or without working in a clinic and seeing outpatients
- ✓ With or without the need for endoscopy
- ✓ Outpatient wound care only
- ✓ Function like an additional partner while a replacement is being found
- ✓ Locations based on temperature variations: Alaska is cool, and Arizona is hot
- ✓ Accommodations for spouses or for one person only
- ✓ Very busy or very slow
- ✓ Trauma center, minimal trauma, or no trauma at all
- ✓ Long-term assignments or one- to two-week assignments
- ✓ Skip a couple of months for a long vacation
- ✓ Work in another country
- ✓ Move to another country and still work in the US one week a month
- ✓ Live in a hotel, apartment, or house
- ✓ Work solo or with a group
- ✓ Big city or small town
- ✓ Large hospital or small community hospital

✓ Fly to assignments or drive

✓ Work only where you have a license already or get an additional license

✓ Go to committee meetings or skip them

✓ Work on an Indian reservation

✓ Work in a Veterans Administration hospital

✓ Work only weekends

✓ Take any holiday off

With so many different options to choose from in the locum tenens world, you can custom design a practice suiting your personality. In my case, I chose to only accept assignments meeting the following criteria: I could drive there, my wife could come with me, low volume workload, little trauma, one to two weeks at a time, and ED call only with no clinic obligations.

These requirements fit what I wanted to do at that stage of my career, which was tapering down my practice to ease into full retirement. You may have different reasons for choosing locum tenens work and consequently would choose different criteria for your ideal assignments. Some want to try out practices before committing to join them. Others would like to live in different parts of the country to test them before moving for good. Whatever your reasoning, take some time to design what would be good for you and stick to your guns. You will be much happier when you choose your ideal work environment rather than taking whatever falls into your lap.

There are dozens of agencies that can connect you to hospitals that need your help. Go to the website of the National Association of Locum Tenens Organizations (NALTO) at nalto.org to find the available companies. Once you contact an agency, you will be assigned to a recruiter who will be your connection for finding assignments. Since each assignment is competitively sought after, they will be relentless in their pursuit of a spot for you. They don't get paid unless you get paid. Answer their emails and phone calls quickly, as these jobs go to the first acceptable candidate and most hospitals put out feelers in several locum tenens agencies to find a good candidate quickly.

As in every profession, the quality of these recruiters varies widely. Look for one who will listen to your needs and will only call you with assignments meeting those needs. If you made it clear you would only consider jobs that allow your spouse to accompany you, and your recruiter calls you about a great job on an island in the Pacific without accommodations for spouses, something is amiss. If they will not work for you and consider your needs, seek another recruiter. There are plenty.

You should sign up with more than one locum tenens agency. If a hospital posts a job with three agencies and you are not with any of them, you will never hear of the job, even if it is only a two-hour drive away. When you do find a good recruiter you love to work with, have them contact all the hospitals near you and present your CV. Then even if a hospital doesn't usually use that agency, you might move to the top of their list since you live so close.

Be sure you know what hospital is asking for help before you commit to doing the job. Some agencies will never tell you this information. The recruiter will say, "A hospital in Idaho." Until they present your name to the hospital, they won't disclose the location. Other agencies will start the conversation with the exact facility and location to consider. When you know exactly what you are deciding on, you will feel very comfortable telling them to present your name to the location. If the recruiter will not show trust in you as a professional, you might consider other options. If you want to know which hospital is asking for help before you say yes, demand it.

Get a feel for why the hospital needs help. It makes a difference if you are covering for a two-month maternity leave versus the only doctor they had just got fired. There is also room for salary negotiation. Just remember, the hospital will take the lowest-priced acceptable candidate. The more desperate they are, the more likely they will increase the offer. When you get called with only two weeks' notice to work for a hospital in which you don't have credentials, you know they are desperate. Sometimes these needs are triggered by an unforeseen circumstance such as an injury.

It is a good idea to work more often at fewer agencies/hospitals/states to cut down on your paperwork. Every new state license and hospital privileges you need to obtain requires another round of paperwork and request for references. Too much of this, and both you and your references will get fed up. For this reason, it is good to have a lot of potential references and rotate them a bit. Do what you can to make it easy on your references. Remember this process will repeat itself every two years when the need to re-credential comes around.

There are so many things you can do to make your time as a locum tenens physician more enjoyable that I put them in a video course, "Thriving in Locum Tenens." You will find this course on my website at DrCorySFawcett.com. If this is the path you choose, do yourself a favor and get the course—your life will be so much better.

Locum tenens can be a nice way to continue to see patients and yet work only as much as you want. If you only take short-term assignments, you can take all the time off you like. Work for a month and take a month off. Then work another place for a month and take another month off.

You can even get really wild and do short assignments at a small hospital, working ten days in a row and flying back home to your condo on the French Riviera for the rest of the month. Now that's the life!

As with everything, consider the downside. Doing locum tenens means you will be traveling a lot. If your spouse works or you have children at home, this may not be the best option. If you don't like change, you may not be happy. Make a list of the pros and cons and find out if this is a good option for you. Then go out and find an assignment that will work for you. The beauty of this method of working is you will be able to try it out without burning any bridges. You can do an assignment on a vacation week and take it for a test drive.

BECOME A SUBSPECIALIST IN YOUR FIELD

If you really want a change in your practice, consider a subspecialty you like within your current expertise, or maybe even become a specialist for a single diagnosis. If you choose something you really enjoy, you will love going to work each day and the demand on your time will be much less with a smaller population segment to see. You can gear all your future CME toward this new subspecialty and become the local expert.

I'm sure you have something in your practice that is a favorite. During your career, you may naturally gravitate to learning more about this topic and preferentially attend CME that covers it, read articles about it, and love to see it on the day's schedule. Early on, it may be just a part of your practice. This special interest has the potential to later become the focus of your practice. How great would your day be if every patient on the schedule was coming to see you about your favorite problem? No more seeing the diagnosis you dread. Every patient would be fun.

For example, a vascular surgeon can cut back to only seeing venous disease and become the local referral doctor for varicose veins. An internist could cut back to only seeing patients with diabetes. An orthopedic surgeon can reduce her practice to only hand surgery cases. In all of these examples, the physicians are already trained to do the subspecialty and simply expanded their patient population with the one favorite diagnosis and eliminated all the other patients with other diagnoses.

Alternatively, instead of limiting your practice to one thing, you could remove something you don't like. As I mentioned earlier, at one point in my career after I became debt-free and gained the courage to make the move, I gave up vascular and thoracic surgery. I only did these cases because they paid well. But every time one of them was on my schedule, I felt the hairs on the back of my neck standing up. I didn't enjoy taking care of those patients but was afraid to give them up because I thought I would lose a substantial portion of my income if I did. When that fear was removed by becoming debt-free, I went for it.

I had one partner who loved vascular surgery and another who loved thoracic surgery. I finally pulled the trigger and had the office staff start diverting those cases away from me and towards the doctors who wanted them. Giving up something I didn't enjoy and transferring those cases to someone who loved them was a win-win deal. As it turned out, my income did not drop. When these cases went on their schedule, something needed to be displaced to make room. Cases I wanted to see were moved to me so they could see these cases they wanted to see. My practice became more enjoyable and so did theirs.

What diagnosis can you drop from your schedule that you don't like? What could you add more of that you do like? Can you get the word out that you want to see those patients with your favorite diagnosis and improve your referral pattern? Even if you are an employed physician, you can control what type of things you have placed on the schedule. Make an effort to take charge of your practice and it will become much more rewarding.

DAVID APPLEBY, MD

I am a retired orthopedist now, and as it was for others of my era, subspecialization was not routinely expected. Residency directors thought it would narrow our capabilities too much. But I felt incompletely trained in hand surgery, so when I was offered a chance to do some extra time focusing on hand and arm surgery, I took it and enjoyed the work. I then joined a group of general orthopedists in a small rural community, far from practices where hand subspecialty was common.

In our town, all orthopedists were generalists. Although I let it be known within weeks of arriving that I would be glad to address the more difficult upper extremity cases, I settled into managing patients with bunions, meniscal tears, and low back pain. And when on call for the ER, I fixed hips and ankles as well as wrists and fingers.

Within about six weeks, I was seeing as many patients in my clinic as I could, but it was not the makeup I had hoped for. I announced to my partners that I did not want to see any more neck and back patients except when on call. That freed me to see more carpal tunnel problems and Dupuytren's Contracture and rotator cuff disease. Gradually over the next couple of years, my reputation as a hand surgeon spread. I was soon seeing patients from the next town (25 miles away). By the start of my third year in practice, I told my partners that I would continue to treat ER patients of all kinds, but I wanted to make my elective practice essentially all hand and arm cases.

My motivation was that I wanted to deal with the problems for which I had developed a special talent and from which I drew more satisfaction. That is just exactly how it played out for several years.

A new pressure arose, though, when I turned 50. Heart problems necessitated three surgeries which left me much more limited than I had been. The cardiac surgeon and cardiologist told me that I should not take ER call anymore for orthopedics. So, I faced a choice of early retirement or restructuring my practice so that I could do less taxing work. Feeling I was too young to retire, I appealed to the hospital and the other orthopedists in town for modification of my privileges and avoidance of ER call. I met with stiff resistance.

As it worked out, I gained permission to work exclusively at a freestanding outpatient surgery center doing hand to elbow cases.

Fortunately, that option was ideal for me. The hand and arm cases, which I loved, were not so physically strenuous (most are done sitting down). I had pared down my practice to patients with a narrower range of problems—those that I particularly enjoyed diagnosing and treating—which would not compromise my health or put me in jeopardy of life-threatening circumstances. And so for the next ten years, I only took hand, wrist, forearm, and elbow cases. With careful planning, I did not have patients admitted to the hospital, and I had a remarkably low incidence of complications.

To my satisfaction, with the change I became a better diagnostician and a better technical surgeon, as my total focus was on that narrower spectrum of problems. Without the burden of ER call, patients waited no more than ten days to see me in consultation and surgery was always done within a week after that. Late nights and long weekends of work were behind me. My family saw me more. My health and state of mind benefited from that normalcy.

In the last five years of my practice, I accepted the part-time role of non-operating upper extremity surgeon working for a group of orthopedists. That final step allowed me to work three days a week or fewer and thereby permitted me to explore activities I would later expand upon in retirement.

By narrowing my focus twice—to outpatient hand surgery and then to non-operative care—I had found a new contentment in my work and my patients were the better for the change. I can recommend this option to anyone looking to redefine their current working situation.

SURGICAL FIRST ASSISTANT

If you are a surgeon or assist in surgery, you could consider cutting back to only assisting. An experienced surgeon makes a great first assistant. A family practitioner who likes to assist and begins doing it more frequently also becomes a great first assistant. Taking call could be an option if you wanted it, but you could avoid it as well. Your availability can be as flexible as you want it to be. You can pick and choose the doctors you like working with and the times you like to work. Many surgeons take this approach as they near retirement as a way to slow down but still have their hand in the operating room, doing what they loved for so many years. Instead of quitting completely, they become first surgical assistants and not necessarily in their specialty. A good surgical assistant can work in any field. They still enjoy the excitement of the operating room, but since they aren't responsible for any patients, their stress level falls several notches.

As a surgical assistant, you can drop all the rest of your hospital privileges. Without other privileges, you will no longer be in the call rotation to cover the emergency department. You will not need an office or any office staff. The surgical office wanting you to assist can call your cell phone directly to schedule your time. You will still have to deal with billing and collecting, in some cases. Some surgeons will hire you directly and they will do the billing, so you can collect your fee from the surgeon directly. Your malpractice insurance rates will drop substantially. You can be in full control of your schedule. When called, you can always say you are not available if you had something special to do like attend your grandchildren's Christmas pageant.

OFFICE PROCEDURES

If you are a surgeon, you can eliminate your hospital privileges and call responsibility and only do minor office surgery. Think about how many cosmetic and simple procedures can be done in the office. Restricting your practice to office surgery can be very rewarding and it offers a much more controlled lifestyle. There are very few night calls and after-hour disturbances in this career option. Not many patients will be dying from having a mole or skin tag removed.

If you want your schedule to be a little more challenging and you have privileges in an outpatient surgery center, you can eliminate all the work requiring a hospital stay and restrict your patient population to those suitable for the surgery center. For example, one internist gave up everything in his practice except screening colonoscopies one day a week at the surgery center. He was able to do this for a few years before retiring completely. He had a long-standing referral pattern that kept him busy until he was finally ready to stop completely. He enjoyed giving up his time in the call schedule.

Malpractice insurance premiums and stress level will both drop as your patient load and complexity decreases. You will likely need fewer office staff employees in this model as well, thus decreasing overhead. Put some good thought into how your new life will look before making the move to be sure you will enjoy the results. If you happen to be a doctor who thrives on the fast-paced lifestyle, slowing down to this level might make you feel like a fish out of water. Be sure to think through your next move carefully before taking the plunge.

MARK DEATHERAGE, MD, FACS

I knew from about age fourteen I wanted to be a doctor, so in my 50s I found that I was a happy and successful general and vascular surgeon who was not interested in retirement. However, as a surgeon ages, some things begin to change. Long operative cases take a toll, and if you are awakened more than once at night, it is difficult to get adequate sleep. That makes the following day's schedule exhausting. I was looking for a way to stay in medicine but without emergency room call.

About that time, the endovascular modalities for venous insufficiency became popular and highly effective. This was a natural subspecialty for a vascular surgeon. I could not only do the procedures, but do all the adjunctive work as well. Furthermore, already having a private office, the startup costs were minimal and it added a new patient stream to our surgical practice.

I started by taking the proprietary vein treatment courses, bought the requisite equipment and began the journey. I traveled to several well-known vein treatment specialists throughout the United States, getting advice on treatment practices, equipment, and marketing. I advertised on television, put on vein seminars, and visited most of the primary care offices, buying them lunch in return for listening to my presentation on the new vein treatments.

As the vein treatment business grew, I backed off on other surgical procedures. At about age 68, I quit taking emergency room call and gave away most of my hospital surgical cases to my younger partner. I still do the outpatient surgical procedures that I enjoy and have one or two endoscopy days a week, but the bulk of my practice is treating venous insufficiency.

I still feel engaged as part of our medical community. I enjoy my time with the medical students and the residents, but don't have to go in at night or receive nightly phone calls. I make it to the gym almost every day and stay fit for my cycling adventures in Italy. Life has definitely gotten better.

CONCIERGE MEDICINE

There are many different ways to structure a medical practice, much like the many different card games that can be played with the same deck of 52 playing cards. Most doctors only consider two of these alternatives: traditional private practice and employment. Other options do exist and come in several different flavors, such as concierge medicine, Ideal Medical Practice clinic, direct medical care, direct primary care, VIP medical care, membership model practices, house call practices, and many others. They all have in common a desire to enhance the doctor-patient relationship by improving access, expediting services, and creating a more pleasant environment for both the patient and the doctor.

According to the Physicians Foundation, 16.4% of physicians surveyed in 2016 plan on transitioning to some type of cash-only practice in the near future, either fully or partially. There are many variables to manipulate: monthly or yearly membership fee, fee for service, accepting insurance, accepting Medicare, limiting the patient population, and making house calls, to name a few.

Why have these options surfaced? Patients and doctors are fed up with the assembly-line practices in many doctor groups today. The pressure to run patients through the office in ten- to fifteen-minute appointment slots and still complete the required charting is not providing enough direct contact between the patient and the doctor. The doctor-patient relationship is suffering and the doctor's ability to provide quality medicine is restricted.

The three elements all customers (patients) want are quick response, quality service, and low price. You can pick any two, but you can never pick all three. Whichever two you choose, the other will not be possible. The concierge medicine model is an attempt to break this rule and get all three aspects at the same time.

For what seems like a relatively low fee, patients have access to a doctor on short notice, and the doctor can give them the time they need. The doctor is able to do this by limiting staff and overhead and taking fewer people into their practice. This model allows doctors to provide better care to fewer patients, and both doctors and patients are happier with the arrangement. Removing the middleman—the insurance companies—from the equation is often a key component. Much of the normal overhead of a practice is centered on dealing with insurance companies and their billing requirements.

Removing the influence of the insurance companies has a profound effect. No one else will be telling you how to practice medicine. No one else will be telling you what you are allowed to charge for your time or when you can do a test or offer a screening exam. For the first time in your career, you can call the shots and no one is between you and your patient.

Often a primary care physician, when compared to the standard practice model either employed or independent, will experience an increase in take-home pay and a decrease in time demanded of them when they convert to one of these business models. Surgeons who are only working out of their office can also operate on a cash-only basis, especially if the services they offer are elective and not covered by most insurance policies anyway.

The driver for the increased number of these clinics is a system making the life of a primary care physician unbearable and underpaid—their time with patients is limited, they are being told how to practice medicine, and they are often paid less than half what a specialist makes. As Dr. Pamela Wible would say, "There is a desire to leave production-driven care and return to relationship-driven care." In a concierge model, you can spend more time with your patients, provide the kind of medical care you want to, and earn a salary similar to a specialist. In some circumstances, patients can combine an insurance policy for catastrophic coverage with a concierge membership for no more than "regular" insurance costs.

If you have an interest in establishing one of the many types of concierge practices, you might consider visiting concierge-medicinetoday.org or idealmedicalcare.org as a starting point.

PAMELA WIBLE, MD

IdealMedicalCare.org

I'm a family physician who was born into a family of physicians. Both my parents are doctors and I went to work with them as a child. My dad actually used to introduce me to his patients as a doctor-in-training before I even entered grade school. I thought it was fun and so I decided early on that I wanted to be one of those docs who could do everything for everyone, so I chose family medicine.

After my training, I found myself funneled into these big-box clinics, and I felt more like a factory worker than a doctor. I was tired of seeing patients in five-minute increments, so in 2005 I left what I call assembly-line medicine and led a series of town hall meetings where I invited my community to design their own ideal medical clinic. I collected more than 100 pages of testimony and adopted 90% of their feedback, and one month later we opened the first ideal clinic designed entirely by patients. For the first time, my job description was written by my patients, not administrators.

As you can imagine, I'm having a lot more fun now. With no administrators or staff, patients enjoy direct 24/7 access to me by phone and email. Appointments are 30 to 60 minutes, scheduled on weekday afternoons and evenings. Sessions begin on time—guaranteed—or patients choose a present from our gift basket. I even do house calls! All of this for no extra fees. Insurance is accepted. Uninsured are welcomed. Best of all, we've never turned anyone away for lack of money. It's a dream come true for me, for my patients, and for my community. Surprisingly (due to my very low overhead) I'm able to make my previous full-time salary working part time.

I absolutely love what I do and I am finally practicing in alignment with the original vision that brought me to medicine. I highly recommend the low-overhead ideal clinic model to anyone in medicine. Solo practice is fun, exciting, and lucrative.

EXPERT WITNESS AND INDEPENDENT MEDICAL EXAMINER

You might envision this option as working for the dark side. As it turns out, most of the cases you review for a plaintiff attorney will lead you to determine there was no medical malpractice committed, so there is no basis on which to file a malpractice suit.

Patients who have complications are taught in our society to blame someone. Blaming the doctor means starting a malpractice suit. We have all seen ads from attorneys looking for clients that say something like, "Did you take drug X and have Y bad outcome? If so, you may be entitled to compensation." Litigation is running rampant.

Once a patient contacts an attorney, the attorney needs a physician to review the chart—for a fee—to see if the case has merit. When you review a case, you generally find one of two things: there was no malpractice, merely a poor outcome, and you tell the plaintiff attorney not to file suit; or, you find the doctor really did not follow the standard of care and caused undue injury, and therefore the patient should be compensated and a suit is warranted. Often, you will be getting a fellow practitioner off the hook—and the rest of the time, you will be sending a message to the doctor that the care rendered was not adequate or in keeping with the standard of care.

In order to do expert witness work properly, you will have to take cases from both plaintiff and defense attorneys to avoid bias. When you review a case for a defense attorney, you will either (1) find a clear defense that refutes the alleged malpractice to assist the defendant or (2) identify that the care was indeed mishandled, so there is no good defense and the best course of action is to settle the case promptly. You need to realize that you will have to clearly explain your opinion (backed up by facts in the record) and may have to write clear reports outlining your opinion, be deposed by the opposing attorney, or testify at trial if you do this work. Each state has different rules that govern expert witnesses. Some states require that you are actively in clinical practice, others require experience in the field, and some just require you to have an active medical license. Many physicians use this work to supplement or even replace some or all of their clinical income. To learn more, go to seak.com/expert-witness-resources. SEAK, Inc. offers courses and other resources such as DVDs and books to get you started in this line of work and to help you excel as an expert witness.

Reviewing malpractice cases is not the only work in this area. Insurance companies and workers compensation companies need independent medical examiners to determine the extent of a patient's disability. Imagine a patient who has been injured, but the insurance company is not giving them disability. You have an opportunity to get someone the disability income they deserve. Or conversely, if someone is faking a disability to defraud the insurance company, you can help stop a fraudulent claim.

Independent medical examiners need to be able to review a chart, possibly examine a patient, and write a clear and concise report about their findings. Sounds a lot like what we do on a day-to-day basis already. This can either become full-time work or could be used to supplement your income and cut back on your regular practice. If you are interested in this, SEAK, Inc. has put together a full course on teaching you how to do this successfully. You can check it out at this site: supplementalincomeforphysicians.com/how-to-start-doing-independent-medical-examinations/.

A.J., MD

Twenty years ago, as a mother with young children, I cut back on my clinical/academic workload by one day per week. With this increased flexibility, I was able to develop an expert witness consulting service in my field of geriatric medicine. I assist both plaintiff and defense attorneys in medical malpractice as well as nursing home and assisted living facility litigation cases. The detective work necessary to study the medical record in detail, discover explanations for what happened, and define if the malpractice allegations were justified was a great change of pace which allowed me to apply my skills in a new way.

Most medical records are sent electronically these days, so this work requires reading large computer files while sitting in front of a computer screen. Digging through the records (often with some background classical music), formulating an unbiased opinion as to whether the physician or facility staff met the standard of care while treating the patient, and then explaining this opinion in clear terms to the attorney who hired me is both fun and challenging for me. As a medical school faculty member teaching geriatric medicine, I now also apply my teaching skills to educating the attorneys (and when necessary, the jury) about the medical aspects of each case, defining my opinion in clear and simple terms. Some of the attorneys are well-versed in medical jargon and quite able to understand everything discussed, while others need everything explained in a more basic way.

Financially, this has been a very beneficial addition for me. As an associate professor also working in the faculty practice doing primary care geriatrics in the outpatient clinic, nursing home, and assisted living facility as well as home visits, my income was at the bottom of the range for specialty physicians. However, by serving as an expert witness, working only one day a week, I was able to double my income. I earn as much in my consulting work one day per week as I make the rest of the week working clinically and teaching! This side gig grew by word of mouth, as one attorney would tell another what a great job I did helping them with a case review. Twenty years later, I have a panel of attorneys all over the country that call me when they have a case in my field of expertise. This has been both an enjoyable and profitable endeavor. I would recommend this sideline to any doctor looking to add a little spice to their career, as all fields are needed for such expert witness work.

MEDICAL MISSIONS AND VOLUNTEER WORK

There are numerous opportunities for a trained doctor to help out in a volunteer capacity. Some states even have a reduced fee license for doing just this. The license will not allow you to be paid for your services, but you will be able to practice your craft for those in need.

There are many organizations that provide medical care to people overseas who do not share the same access to medical care we have in this country. Most of them will require you to have an active license to practice. These can be very rewarding experiences.

You also don't need to have a passport to help the less fortunate. There are many ways to provide healthcare in your own state to those in need. Many free clinics can use the help of someone with your experience. I set up a clinic at my local Gospel Rescue Mission to see patients once a week on site. The patients were grateful, the staff at the mission were grateful, and the doctors who came and volunteered their time were glad to have a way to give back.

If you are interested in this area you can search the Internet for medical volunteer sites. Some good places to start are Health Volunteers Overseas, Doctors Without Borders, and Mercy Ships. If you put the word out that you are interested in volunteer work, you are likely to find other colleagues who have the same interest and have already done some research or been on a mission trip and can point you in the right direction.

There are many other ways to continue practicing medicine in a new or reduced capacity. Often, this is all you need. You have valid reasons for thinking about retirement, but consider how you would feel if you could work in one of these alternatives. Look around for an opportunity and follow a new path. It will be a refreshing new chapter in your life. You will also still feel like a doctor.

Chapter 4

NONCLINICAL CAREER ALTERNATIVES

The Physicians Foundation survey of 2016 found that 13.5% of the doctors they surveyed were planning on transitioning into some sort of nonclinical position, up from 10.4% two years earlier. There has been an increasing exodus of physicians from clinical practice over the last several years. What other future besides providing medical care could a doctor have?

Contrary to popular belief, your doctorate is useful for more than seeing patients in exchange for money. There are many other ways to use your knowledge and experience. Your choices are broader than retiring to play golf or continuing in a different type of medical practice. Nonclinical positions that use your knowledge, degree, and experience are quite possible to find and enable you to have a complete change of pace.

If you are interested in a nonclinical medical career, you should look into attending the SEAK, Inc. Non-Clinical Careers for

Physicians conference, usually held in October. You can meet people who have successfully gone into nonclinical careers and ask them questions. Recruiters are there looking for doctors for specific opportunities. Look for more information on seak.com or nonclinicalcareers.com.

The nonclinical career options for doctors have a little bit of stigma associated with them. You will have colleagues tell you, "After training for so long, you are throwing it all away. What a waste." Your friends and relatives might say the same. You may wonder if you will still feel like a "doctor." But I assure you, you are still a doctor. You are not throwing away your education. Building on the platform of your medical knowledge, you can serve many more people in the nonclinical areas than you could ever serve seeing individual patients one at a time.

A private practice physician might touch the lives of 30 patients a day. As the administrator of a health plan, you might affect 10,000 people a day. The scope of your ability to help people will grow. You will have the ability to make life better for those who are working in the trenches and seeing the patients one on one. If you can enable clinical doctors to practice longer, more efficiently, or safer, your influence can be tremendous. Improving quality and utilization will have a big impact.

Another area doctors are concerned about in a nonclinical career is a potential cut in pay. Doctors seeing patients make a good living, but they also pay a high price in the forms of overloaded schedules and stressful work, which cuts into their lifestyle and family time. Call nights, weekends away from the family, and the stress of critical patients and malpractice suits can take a toll. The high divorce and suicide rates among those in our noble profession bear that out. In some nonclinical areas, you will likely take a cut in pay; in others, you can experience a significant pay increase. In all of them, you will experience a drastic lifestyle improvement.

Doctors in general are organized, resourceful, efficient, intelligent, dedicated, and dependable. They are problem-solvers and leaders with a good work ethic. You have many skills to offer an employer beyond your degree. There are many nonclinical areas available for someone with your background, knowledge, and abilities. Let's take a look at a few of them.

MEDICAL INFORMATICS

There is a tremendous push to computerize everything in medicine.

✓ Databases: Epocrates, Medscape, UpToDate . . .

✓ Diagnostics: Cybermed, Orthanc, VistA imaging . . .

✓ EHR: Epic, MEDITECH, Allscripts . . .

✓ Laboratory: eLab, STARLIMS, webLIMS . . .

✓ Practice management: Kareo, ClearHealth, Dentrix . . .

These are but a few of the areas medical informatics, or medical information technology (IT), has invaded.

Physicians are needed to help in the development of these programs, as well as teaching others to efficiently use them and integrate them into their practice. The companies developing these systems need the input of doctors who will be using their programs to make them more efficient. Hospitals and clinics purchasing the programs need instructors to teach the most efficient ways to use the systems. Government agencies need to interface with the private sector, and doctors can be a vital part of making that interface work.

When a hospital spends $5 million purchasing a new EHR system, they want the transition to go smoothly. Who better to hire than a physician consultant who not only knows how to best utilize the new system, but can also speak as a colleague to the users? A recent search on LinkedIn for "Epic consultant" resulted in 5955 hits. A search for "physician Epic consultants" found 645. Not all of these consultants were physicians; some were listed as consultants to physicians, but many had Dr. or MD beside their names.

Integrating medical practices with social media is becoming very popular as well. With each new social medial platform, more immediate access to doctors becomes possible. We live in a "right now" society, and developing applications to connect patients with their doctors quickly is needed. Consultants are needed to modernize the connectivity doctors have with their patients and to integrate computers with smart phones and tablets to make medical practices more mobile. Doctors can now make rounds from home and check patients' vital signs, labs, and imaging studies before setting foot in the hospital.

When I was in medical school, I didn't see the IT area as a career possibility, so who knows where we will be in another ten years? Doctors will always be needed to help make these systems relevant and useful. If you can save a practice hundreds of hours in their implementation, you are valuable. Time is money.

If you have a special spot in your heart for technology, this might be the place for you. Meld your medical knowledge with technological advances to establish a whole new type of medical communications for the future. Simply do a google search for the area you are most interested in to find a list of companies in that field. Then go to each company website and find the HR contact person and send them an email about your interest in the company and what you might be able to provide. You will discover their level of interest and go from there. If one company is not interested, move down your list.

When I searched for electronic health record companies, I found 497 companies specializing in private practices and 159 companies working with hospitals. There were some overlaps in the two lists but it should give you an idea of the vast scope of opportunities in the medical IT field.

EDUCATION AND RESEARCH

Medical, osteopathic, dental, and other schools need instructors, many of whom will no longer see patients. Someone needs to teach the next generation of students anatomy and physiology. Whichever organ system or specialty you have the greatest experience with could be your area of teaching expertise. Now your years of experience become very valuable, without the need to deal with insurance companies or take any call.

You can become a clinical investigator and spend your time doing research and working in the lab. In this role, you would be putting out papers and establishing the future of medicine. Who knows what discoveries are awaiting you? Is there a particular niche you are interested in? If you go to work every day doing something you love—your niche—you never really go to work, you go to have fun and discover new and exciting things.

Contact schools and research institutes fitting your area of interest and you just might find your dream job awaiting.

MEDICAL COMMUNICATIONS

The field of medical communications is rapidly expanding. The ability to use social media in medicine is expanding exponentially. Online resources include teaching videos, blogs for doctors and patients, and handouts used for patient education. You can also find Online courses for patient safety and for teaching hospitals how to comply with the latest new government mandate. Physicians can play key roles in imparting knowledge to others by preparing this content.

A LinkedIn search as of this writing for "medical communications" found 985 contacts of groups, companies, and job offers. There were opportunities in government agencies, private consulting firms, large hospital systems, companies providing medical information for patients, CME companies, and so much more.

You have developed many useful skills over your career and if this area is a passion, put those skills to good use.

KEVIN PHO, MD

KevinMD.com

I entered the medical field with a desire to guide patients through our complicated healthcare system as their advocate. I loved hearing all the personal stories and helping solve their medical issues. Since I like to have my hand in everything, specialization did not suit my personality and I fit right in with being a general internist. It is not without its challenges, but overall I have found my career in medicine to be very rewarding and there is nothing else I would rather do.

In 2004 I launched a new endeavor, KevinMD, to give physicians a voice in healthcare in the same way I did with my patients. I began with a blog and a social media presence for fellow physicians. Policies and decisions were being made by people who were not in the exam room. Frontline physicians needed a venue where they could tell their story, voice an opinion, and express what needed to change and improve in our healthcare system. Social media was young then, and I had no guidebook to tell me how to do this so I blazed my own trail. Today there are many examples to follow for those wishing to enter the social media realm.

Having another passion besides medicine has helped me avoid the all-too-common problem of physician burnout. Having a way to change gears during the day has kept medicine fresh for me and helped me attain balance in my life. A typical day for me is to rise at 5:00 a.m. and do two hours of writing, editing, and reading other physicians' stories. I then change gears and see patients from about 8:00 a.m. to 3:00 p.m. Then I get to pick up my kids from school and invest a few hours in family time. By 8:00 p.m., I am ready to do some more writing and preparation for speaking events.

Being social media's leading physician voice has been very rewarding. Instead of being limited to the experiences here in New Hampshire, I have been able to hear stories from physicians all across the country and have come to know we are very much alike. We all have the same dreams and face the same challenges. I would have never experienced that without this second passion.

If you are thinking about entering the social media world of communications, I would advise you to first define your mission. Are you planning to educate patients, connect with physicians, fight for a cause, or help reform healthcare? Each mission requires a different approach, and if your initial trajectory is good, your final outcome will be as well.

I'm looking forward to many more years of a happy career in medicine as well as continuing with my other passion of giving a voice to physicians all across the nation.

PHARMACEUTICAL INDUSTRY

The pharmaceutical industry is a blend between business and science. You can play a big role with your experience in the science aspect of this industry. Profit is made when a drug is developed that improves some aspect of health in a safe and cost-effective manner, and a company can convince both doctors and patients to use it. There are several phases of a drug's development, and doctors can play a role all along that continuum.

Early on, new drugs must be assessed for side effects and metabolism, excretion, and dosing. Studies to evaluate these and prove the drug's safety must be designed and conducted. Someone with your background will need to oversee and develop these studies.

Later the safety, efficacy, and side effects will need to be established in different patient groups such as pediatric, obstetric, and geriatric populations. Oversight and structure of these studies must be coordinated by someone with medical knowledge and experience.

Once a good drug is established, someone needs to convince the regulatory agencies it is safe and a useful and effective addition to the medications already on the market. The credibility of a doctor is needed for this. If you have political aspirations, you can become a lobbyist, who is simply a liaison between the business and the politics of pharma.

Without the involvement of doctors, it is unlikely we would have new medication on the market. Your impact could be worldwide. Developing vaccines, stopping heart disease, and treating cancer on a global scale are all possible. That is not the usual activity of a small-town family physician. Your medical degree could impact the world.

There are currently more than 200 pharmaceutical companies in the United States and United Kingdom, all looking for people just like you who are ready to help in such areas as:

✓ Medical directors, who help with the design of clinical trials and development of scientific educational materials.

✓ Medical science liaisons, helping with education of other healthcare professionals, marketing, and promotion.

✓ Clinical research associates, working on design of studies, enrollment of study subjects, data collection, and support of trials and presentations.

✓ Drug safety

✓ Regulatory issues in complying with FDA guidelines

✓ Sales (who better to promote a new blood pressure medication than a cardiologist?)

Pick the area most intriguing to you and do some Internet searches, and you will find more than enough information. Contact companies you have an interest in and begin exploring the possibilities.

HEALTH INSURANCE INDUSTRY

Pleasant thoughts are not what comes to mind for most doctors when discussing the health insurance industry. Instead, they think of rejected requests for care and having to fight for the right to give a patient a therapy they and the patient have already agreed upon.

So why would you want to work in this field? Because that preconceived notion is very skewed and not representative of the job, and you can make a big impact on patient care.

As a society, we have to face the fact that healthcare dollars are limited and must be allocated in ways to help the most people with the dollars available. On the other hand, health-care expenses can be almost unlimited. With a huge pull on limited resources, utilization decisions must be made—there is no way around this fact. When a request does not fit into the defined insurance contract (the treatments and procedures the company contracted with the patient to cover), the possibility of making an exception exists. Computer algorithms take care of the first step in this process, but cases that are kicked out of the system need the review of a real live person.

Doctors and nurses get involved at this step and review each case to be sure it meets standards of care, as well as setting up the algorithms in the first place. An example would be establishing a process to verify screening colonoscopies are not taking place more often than every ten years. If they were being performed at eight-year intervals instead of ten, the cost would increase by 20% without an improvement in overall health. Someone needs to help set the initial standards. Then, if a requesting physician wants to do a colonoscopy sooner than ten years and can justify the need, it would be reasonable to make an exception for that patient. You can use your expertise to be sure people are getting the healthcare they need, without driving up the cost by doing unnecessary procedures. It isn't a matter of denying care, it's more about assuring the right care is given at the best cost.

Handling medical insurance appeals can be done in a government position working with Medicare and Medicaid issues, a position within an insurance company, or even as a third-party independent reviewer. Often a company will look for an outside, independent reviewer to approve or deny a claim, and you could be that person.

You might move up from utilization review to medical director. Here you could be involved in setting healthcare policy in the company. Having a background in medical care is important for this position. Moving up from there you could become the vice president of medical affairs and later even the CEO. Who better to run a health insurance company than a doctor who knows what the insurance should be covering? Directing medical care can produce a higher salary than providing medical care. That is not the way it should be, but that's the way it is.

If you are involved with utilization or even case management, you may be able to work from home, avoiding the need to relocate. Working from your home office via phone and computer, while dressed in your bathrobe and without a beeper or the risk of malpractice, can be very appealing. You might not have any direct patient contact, but you will still be affecting patient care. If this interests you, start contacting healthcare insurance agencies near you and discuss what they might have available.

CONSULTING

The rapidly changing healthcare industry has created many opportunities for consultants to help people and organizations navigate the changes. This has been going on for a very long time. Over 2,500 years ago, the philosopher Heraclitus stated:

> There is nothing more constant than change.

How right he was. With each new invention, government regulation, EHR system, and medical discovery, a built-in need exists for someone to teach other doctors how to work it into their busy lives. If that someone is another doctor in your field, you will feel a natural connection with him or her. He or she has gone through what you have gone through and shares your experiences, and will therefore come across as much more credible in your daily practice.

I remember when the hospital brought in an expert to teach us how to dictate our medical records so payment would be made appropriately. One example he provided was that stating the patient's *temperature* was 104.5 has no code, but if you state the patient has a *fever* of 104.5, you will be paid. There is a code for "fever" but no code for "temperature." If no one ever tells you how it actually works, you don't get paid. Maybe that is exactly the reason it is so complex. I learned a lot at his lecture and I would not have gone if the speaker hadn't been a general surgeon. I knew I could relate to him since we were of the same specialty. As a surgeon himself, the speaker understood how I approached charting and could therefore offer practical advice to maximize payment.

There are numerous other opportunities for doctors to serve as consultants. Here are some additional examples of in-demand knowledge and skills:

✓ Proper coding for the newest version of the International Classification of Diseases, ICD-10

✓ Effective use of EHR systems

✓ Setting up a particular procedure efficiently at an ambulatory surgery center

✓ Complying with HIPAA regulations

✓ Setting up a concierge/ideal medical practice

✓ Preparing a hospital for a mass shooter situation and natural disasters

✓ Passing a joint commission inspection

✓ Applying surgical care improvement project (SCIP) measures to your practice

✓ Developing good physician-hospital relations

✓ Operating room efficiency

✓ Medical architectural design

✓ Medical legal consultant to physicians

Some of these opportunities will be in conjunction with a large organization, i.e., you are employed by a big company to help their employees or customers. In other situations, you can become your own independent consultant. The sky is the limit on this one, as any area where you have expertise—and that someone is willing to pay to learn—becomes a consulting opportunity.

MICHELLE MUDGE-RILEY, DO, MHA, RD, LD, CLT

phphysicians.com

I was in the fourth grade when I told my dad I wanted to become a doctor. Of course, he was thrilled and my entire family supported me throughout my schooling. The day I got accepted to medical school, I felt like my life was finally beginning. Now I was going to be a *doctor*—my dream was coming true.

I did well in medical school (Sigma Sigma Phi honor society) but slowly realized that seeing patients day after day (the description of the job, right?) wasn't what I wanted to do for the next forty years. But I still loved medicine! What was I going to do?

It was a difficult time for me because I didn't know what my options were. Eventually, I went back to school and got a degree in Health Administration, then convinced a company to hire me as their Director of Wellness. That was my first success at being an entrepreneur. I had essentially created an idea and found someone to buy it.

When I started talking about my disenchantment with medicine and how I had found a solution, my story was published in several different places and I was invited to speak about my experiences and about the state of healthcare. That led to other doctors asking me to help them. The entrepreneur in me saw another opportunity, and a year later I started my first company, a physician coaching company. Eight years after that, I started my second company.

Now I am the Entrepreneur in Residence for Trinity University and working on starting my third company. Being a physician entrepreneur is kind of like doing ten jobs at once. I coach people (physicians and nonphysicians), I consult with various hospitals and organizations, and I network with investors and other entrepreneurs. I chase various ideas and projects because not everything works out, but the ones that do are exciting, fun, and lucrative. Physicians have a huge opportunity to invent and innovate, and for me, being an entrepreneur allows me to use my medical background to help many people. With so many physicians looking to reinvent themselves, I began helping them through that process with my consulting business, Physician's Helping Physicians. I love what I do.

MEDICAL DEVICE DEVELOPMENT

Many doctors are closet inventors. You may have ideas floating around in your head for how to improve routine processes
or procedures, or products to solve problems doctors and the
healthcare industry may face. I once built a device to remove
large rectal foreign bodies and presented it at a meeting after
removing the largest-diameter object in the literature. That tool
was built out of necessity on the operating table, and it worked.
I thought about developing the idea, but never went forward
with it. I decided there was not a big enough market for sales.
How many doctors have similar devices in their heads that are
never developed?

What will it take to get a great idea out of your head and
on the market? Taking the extra step of developing your idea
could mean millions in royalties, not to mention the thousands of patients who benefit. A few devices come to mind,
such as the Starr-Edwards heart valve, the Fogarty arterial
embolectomy catheter, and the Greenfield Vena Cava Filter.
Someone came up with the idea for every medical device on
the market. When you are on the frontline of patient care,
you can see how things might be done better or can envision a
device to make your job easier.

The key to success is to take the first step. Don't leave the idea
bouncing around in your head. Move forward and take it to

market. Yes, there is effort involved but the reward can be huge. Not all the ideas will be successful and not all the successful ones will be marketable. Nothing ventured, nothing gained. Taking a product from idea to market requires capital, but the funding doesn't all need to come from you. If you take a good idea to a company making something similar, they may partner with you in the deal. They also have all the infrastructure to make it happen.

You can find more information at eurekamed.com or sopenet.org (The Society of Physician Entrepreneurs).

MEDICAL WRITER

For many doctors, the only thing that comes to mind in this category is writing bestselling novels like Michael Crichton, Robin Cook, and Michael Palmer have done. There are many nonfiction topics that need a doctor's credibility.

Potential areas include writing manuscripts, grant proposals, medical news articles, continuing medical education material, patient information, regulatory reports, medical blogs, and nonfiction books on a wide variety of healthcare topics. Companies publishing books about health topics intended for laypeople often require a "technical editor," which can be a physician in that field who can make sure the information in the book is medically accurate and up to date.

Many doctors have a knack and desire for writing, and you can try it out without giving up your practice. You can begin writing while still practicing medicine and see what happens. Many start with a blog and begin to develop a following. You can write articles for journals, magazines, newspapers, and other people's blogs, and gradually get into the business. Writing about something you have a passion for can improve your chances for success. Who knows, you might even write a classic novel that becomes a movie.

The website contena.co lists available writing gigs, and the first one on that list was for an Oncology Care Writer/Editor. I also looked on upwork.com and searched for "physician writer" and found numerous options. Snoop around for opportunities. You can explore this field risk-free.

JAMES M. DAHLE, MD

WhiteCoatInvestor.com

I have always loved to write. As a teenager, I had interest in three careers: being a physician, being a writer, and operating large excavation equipment. I have been blessed to have had success in two of those three fields so far.

In college, medical school, and even into residency I had very little interest in business or finance. I was a molecular biology major, but mostly I was only interested in science insomuch as it related to medicine. In medical school, emergency medicine became a rather obvious fit for my personality, interests, and aptitude, so I matched into a respected emergency medicine residency program. Like many doctors, I took the recommendation of a fellow resident for a financial advisor who proceeded to sell me some insurance and investments. On a vacation near the end of my intern year, I read my first financial book, *Mutual Funds for Dummies* by Eric Tyson (John Wiley & Sons), and soon discovered that I had mistaken a "fee-based" advisor for a "fee-only" advisor. This was not the first time I felt ripped off by someone in the financial services industry. I previously had bad interactions with an insurance agent, a realtor, and a lender. This encounter, however, was the straw that broke the camel's back.

I lived next to a used bookstore, and with my limited time I began to read every financial book I could get my hands on. Many were poorly written but a few were excellent, and after a while I realized this personal finance and investing stuff wasn't that hard. In fact, the subject matter was far easier than medicine. I took control of my own investments and began functioning as my own financial planner and investment manager. I continued to read books and blogs and to participate on Internet forums. What resulted was a pretty good education in a completely different field than medicine. After a few years, I realized I was doing a lot more teaching than learning online, and also became interested in developing sources of passive income to supplement my clinical income. And I was sick of typing the same thing into the Internet forums over and over again. The White Coat Investor blog was born! Now I could just paste in a URL to a previously written blog post. Just like "Dr. Google" could teach me all kinds of things about personal finance, he could also teach me about blogging professionally.

It took a few years for me to build up a significant readership and to learn how to monetize it effectively, but eventually the blog income became significant—equaling and then finally exceeding my clinical income. My readers encouraged me to write a book. Once more, Dr. Google and some good books showed me how to write, self-publish, and market a book. The blog readers also made huge contributions to the success of *The White Coat Investor: A Doctor's Guide to Personal Finance and Investing,* and it remained at the top of its Amazon categories even three years after publication.

While my intent was never to replace my clinical work by becoming a writer, and I only recently cut back to three-quarter time in the ED, having two solid options to provide for my family has provided a lot of financial security. There is a synergy between the two careers, because each helps me to enjoy and be more effective at the other.

ADMINISTRATION

If you see opportunities to improve the management of your organization and understand how to work within the system, an administrative position may have real potential for you. Ideally, the leader of a healthcare organization or related industry should be someone who has been in the trenches and has actually done what the organization is supposed to do.

In an article from the *Mayo Clinic Proceedings* in April of 2015 titled "Impact of Organizational Leadership on Physician Burnout and Satisfaction" by Shanafelt et al., the authors reported on the effect the leaders of physicians have on the satisfaction and burnout rate of those who are led. For every one-point increase in the leadership score attributed to the "boss," there was a 3.3% decrease in burnout and a 9% increase in satisfaction in the "worker."

There is a better likelihood of empathy from a boss who has trudged through the same trenches you have. There is often a tension between the doctors and the administrators that gains some relief when the administrator is "one of us." Doctors have a potential unfair advantage in developing a collaborative and cohesive environment in an organization that the nonphysician CEO will never enjoy when coming solely from a business background instead of a medical background.

Unfortunately, physician leadership is not common in US hospitals. Gunderman and Kanter stated in their 2009 *Academic Medicine* article (84:1348-1351), titled "Educating Physicians to Lead Hospitals," that of the nearly 6,500 hospitals in the US, only 235 were run by physicians—less than 4%.

Amanda Goodall published an article titled "Physician-Leaders and Hospital Performance: Is There an Association?" in *Social Science & Medicine* (Volume 73, Issue 4, August 2011, pp. 535–539). She looked at the top 100 hospitals in the specialties of cancer, digestive disorders, and heart and heart surgery as published by *US News and World Report's* "Best Hospitals" of 2009. When cross-referencing this list with the CEO's training, namely a physician at the helm vs. a nonphysician, she found physician-run hospitals had quality scores about 25% higher than those run by nonphysicians. When she looked at only the so-called "Honor Roll" hospitals, 16 of 21 (76%) were headed by physicians. She concluded, "hospitals positioned higher in the *US News and World Report's* "Best Hospitals" ranking are led disproportionately by physicians."

Is it possible that CEOs who are MDs may have more experience to make the hard decisions about quality patient care? Of course they do! They have been in the trenches and have a better understanding about patient needs than a nonphysician would have.

Dr. Leslie Ogden, CEO of Samaritan North Lincoln Hospital in Lincoln City, Oregon, was kind enough to sit down with me and discuss her transition from practicing physician to hospital CEO for the companion interviews for this book. Dr. Ogden, an emergency medicine physician, felt she had an advantage over nonphysician CEOs because she could put on scrubs and go into the operating room and look at a problem from a different prospective. She could also accompany nurses taking care of patients and see firsthand what the issues were and therefore get a better handle on how to fix them. A nonphysician CEO would need to rely on secondhand reports of what is happening and would be unable to "get her hands wet." Her unique background makes her more suitable to better evaluate the situation.

Hospital administrators should be physicians who have a special interest in business administration. Can you imagine what our military would be like if the generals were chosen from an applicant pool of business owners who had never served in the military?

There are many organizations that need the leadership of a doctor. I've already mentioned hospitals. There are also medical and dental societies, surgery centers, dental schools, licensing boards, accountable care organizations, state hospital associations, large medical practices, and various types of health plans.

Several administrative positions are available in these organizations: CEO, medical director, chief medical officer, and vice presidents of various sections, such as network development, care management, quality management, and infection control. A doctor who has a knack for business or communication has what it takes to excel in administration.

GOVERNMENT AGENCIES

There are many opportunities in government for doctors. At the federal level, doctors work in several departments, including but not limited to state, defense, health and human services, energy, education, veterans affairs, and NASA. At the state level, doctors are hired for positions in health departments, social services, occupational health services, licensing boards, and labor departments, to name a few. You can find opportunities in public health, emergency response, and global health. There are also local government offices in need of physicians such as county health departments and coroner offices.

If politics is more your thing, as a doctor you are a sought-after commodity as a senator or representative at the state or federal level, as well as in many of the government offices from president on down. The recent 114th Congress of the United States included seventeen physicians; three were senators and fourteen were representatives. Involvement with formulating government regulations in healthcare would be a natural fit. Some political offices are full time and some are part time, but a call schedule is not usually part of the job description.

In summary, many opportunities in nonclinical areas exist for doctors, and many of those areas would benefit greatly from your experience in the healthcare field. Think about what areas you have special interest in. There are many more nonclinical areas than I covered here—however, I hope these ideas inspire you to investigate your own options. SEAK, Inc. also offers many other services to doctors exploring alternatives to a conventional use of their medical degree. It was their influence that helped me see an opportunity as a physician writer and coach. There are also areas to explore that are not connected to your degree such as owning a brewery, running a farm, or even starting a rock-n-roll band. You have unlimited potential.

Chapter 5

ONE ATTRACTIVE CHOICE: ASSISTING IN CRITICAL ACCESS HOSPITALS

After leaving my general surgery practice of twenty years, I spent three years working part time in nearby critical access hospitals (CAHs) before stopping clinical medicine altogether to concentrate on helping other doctors. It was both rewarding and relaxing. I believe this method of reducing your work schedule can have such a big impact for rural America that I decided to devote an entire chapter to this one opportunity. You can end your full-time practice and work part time one to two weeks a month for a nearby CAH to relieve an overworked doctor.

According to the Association of American Medical Colleges' March 2015 report, the US has a physician deficit of about 21,800 and growing. They estimated this shortage will triple by 2020. This shortage is skewed towards rural America. If retiring doctors were to spend the last few years of their careers helping out in rural America, a great impact could be made on the perceived doctor shortage.

You can simply put feelers out in the surrounding small hospitals and see who is interested in your help. Interview for this the same way you would have done getting your first job out of training. Check out the town, the housing, and the hospital facilities, and most of all meet the doctor you will be covering. It is good to learn something of the style of the doctor who works there and not throw too many curves at the staff. Everyone is used to the way "their doctor" does things, and the closer you can mirror that, the better.

There are several advantages and disadvantages to this option, and I would like to give you perspectives on a few of them.

ADVANTAGES

FEELING USEFUL

The biggest and most important advantage for me was feeling useful. I was able to use my skills, honed over the years, to make a contribution to society and my self-worth. The community I worked for during my twenty-year practice had ten general surgeons; they really didn't need me anymore.

Three of the CAHs I helped had only one general surgeon, who was never off the pager. These doctors were very grateful for my help, as it allowed them to have some much-needed downtime. The hospital administrators voiced their thanks for having me on a regular schedule so they didn't need to worry about coverage when their lone surgeon needed time off. "I know a good thing when I see it," was one administrator's comment about our arrangement. This was refreshing; praise and thanks were lacking in the larger hospital where I had worked for twenty years.

The hospital staff were also very thankful for my help. They knew their surgeon was overworked and overstressed, and they didn't want to lose him. They understood the significance of my work in helping their surgeon stay healthy so he could continue working in their community. Without someone to help him, there was a good chance he would eventually leave, and they knew he would be hard to replace. Without a general surgeon, the hospital and the patients would suffer significantly.

SLOWER PACE

After twenty years of practice, I wanted to cut back significantly on the hours I worked. The arrangement I made with the CAHs was to cover the hospital's on-call needs for a week. This meant I didn't have any other obligations. I had no scheduled appointments in the office. I had no scheduled elective surgeries. I was on no committees. I only covered for the emergency department calls, consults from other physicians, and patients who called in after hours. CAHs are located in rural areas and with the lower populations they serve, the number of emergencies was significantly less compared to what I was used to seeing in my busy practice. Consequently, I had a lot of free time while I was working.

Another aspect of slowing the pace was being away from home. My house surrounds me with "things to do." I look out the window and see a bush that needs trimming. The stack of periodicals on my desk needs to be read. A loose doorknob can use some attention. My garage is a mess. We rented a sparsely furnished apartment to use when I worked in these small towns, and when I awoke in the morning, I looked around and could not see any "things to do."

This new free time allowed me to do things that had been missing from my earlier, busy life. My wife and I were able to ride our tandem bicycle, although we couldn't stray too far from home as I needed to be able to respond to the ED if needed. We explored the town during business hours. We did the grocery shopping together. I worked on projects like writing this book. I had more time to read. My wife and I had more free time together.

NO OVERHEAD

One of the challenges I faced when trying to cut back the workload in my private practice partnership was meeting my share of the overhead expenses. As I slowed down, my production fell but my share of the overhead did not fall correspondingly. Consequently, my take-home pay took a big hit when I began working fewer hours and traveling more.

In private practice, overhead costs can be a limiting factor to working part time since most of these costs are fixed, and you are responsible for covering them. This is the same reason employed doctors encounter resistance when trying to work part time. The employer will still need to cover those fixed overhead expenses and you will not be producing as much money to do so. Overhead expenses are always present in every practice model—only the party responsible for the costs changes with the models.

In my new position as an employee at a CAH, I had no office overhead. When I wasn't working, my income simply fell to zero—it didn't go negative as it would in my private practice. The negative cash flow issue caused by practice overhead is very worrisome to many doctors when they consider taking a vacation. During vacation, their practice overhead continues and income production stops. Some doctors even send their family on vacation while they stay home to continue production in order to pay their overhead. This entire issue of negative cash flow was eliminated under my new CAH arrangement.

PAID TRAVEL

My wife and I always went to my assignments together. Since we would go by car and the CAH hospital paid my travel expenses and accommodations, we were essentially on an all-expenses-paid vacation. I only accepted assignments to locations we wanted to see, so it really was like a vacation with a little bit of work thrown in. I averaged a little under one new patient a day, since my only source of patients was a small-town emergency department and there was no office time scheduled.

There were several remote areas within driving distance of our home that we had not visited and had a CAH in need of my services. I might not otherwise have picked that location for a vacation, but it still had sights to offer. If someone was to pay me to travel there, it was worth visiting. You can also stay a few extra days before or after the assignment and see the surrounding area.

One such example was a small town on the Olympic Peninsula in Washington. We had never been there, despite having lived in the Pacific Northwest our entire lives. I covered for one missing surgeon, but this CAH had a total of three surgeons, and the other two were still working. That meant I was not on call every day. On the off-call days, with no elective schedule, my wife and I were able to go hiking in the nearby rain forest. We were also able to visit all the nearby towns we would not have seen otherwise. We had a great time. And our housing and travel were covered in the contract.

STILL EARNING INCOME

This may be a big factor for you. Maybe you haven't saved enough during your earning years to be without earned income, yet you would like to significantly cut back or retire.

Also, retirement plans are not easily accessible before age 59½ without paying a tax penalty, although there is a way to work around those penalties by using tax rule 72(t), as I will explain in the chapter The Financial Phases of Your Life, but the requirements might not be to your liking. Supplementing your income with a less stressful part-time job during this period can be of great benefit. This might mean the difference between semi-retirement now versus having to wait until you've saved the magic number in the retirement plan or you reach age 59½, for hassle-free withdrawals.

Supplementing your income for a few more years while allowing your retirement accounts to continue growing without any withdrawals can produce a lot of additional growth in those accounts. Time is your friend while you are collecting interest, and a part-time job could buy you a lot of time for that interest to compound.

THE IMPACT A FEW YEARS OF PART-TIME WORK CAN HAVE

As an example, suppose your retirement plan has a balance of $1 million and has been growing at 8% a year—a conservative average. Working part time for three more years without making any more deposits to the account will allow it to grow to $1,259,712. This extra quarter of a million dollars would produce an additional $10,388 per year of retirement income over the $40,000 per year it would have produced if you used a 4% annual withdrawal rate. That amounts to approximately a 25% increase in your retirement income by simply stalling for three years before beginning to live on the income. So staying productive, getting a "paid" vacation, and living a more relaxing life just boosted your retirement income by 25%. Not a bad trade.

HANDING OFF DIFFICULT PATIENTS

We have all picked up the long-term patient while on call. They have a problem requiring several weeks of hospitalization. This means even when you are not on call anymore, you have a patient in the hospital. That patient will need rounding, phone calls, and charting. Since as a stand-in you will work for a set number of days—usually one to two weeks—you can hand off the difficult patient at the end of the assignment and be totally free from obligations.

If you chose to work two weeks in a row but at separate hospitals, you will be able to sign out and start with a clean slate at the second hospital. Long-term patients in the hospital are a bit of a drain on your energy level. Being able to hand off those cases and start over with no patients the next day is very freeing.

DISADVANTAGES

Everything has its downside and there are a few disadvantages to this method of working as well. Here are a few you might experience.

YOU ARE NOT AT HOME

All of the activities you have at home, such as friends, gym membership, and bridge club are not available when you travel. If you commit to working at two hospitals and providing one week a month coverage for each of them, then you will be away from home for at least two weeks a month.

Anything you want to do on a weekly basis will be interrupted. If you want to take weekly dance classes, you will miss half of them. Things around the house will not get done and will begin to pile up almost as fast as the incoming mail. Someone must be hired to keep up the yard if you were doing it yourself, so you don't come home to an overgrown jungle. Your friends will not be readily available. You may be away from your grown children and their families. If you have rental property you will need to hire a property management company.

In my case, I initially loved the traveling. Later, I began to miss the things at home we gave up in order to travel. Everything has its trade-offs—I gave up some time at home. But as I mentioned under the Advantages section, I traded for more free time to write and enjoy time with my wife, while still earning an income and using my skills.

INCREASED PAPERWORK

Each hospital you work for requires credentialing paperwork, which must be renewed every two years. Each new hospital is another application. Each new state is another license. Some states also require prescription credentialing. Every insurance panel requires credentialing. Granted, these only happen periodically, but the more hospitals you work with, the more frequent these credentialing events become. There are ways to streamline this and decrease the hassle factor.

If you work for a locum tenens company, they will do some of the paperwork for you. But to hear them talk about it, they are doing it all for you. There is still a lot for you to do. Continually asking your colleagues to write another letter of recommendation to yet another hospital is also not desirable for you or them. Consequently, it is better to use fewer hospitals and return more often, rather than many hospitals with occasional assignments. The repeat customers make the paperwork less onerous. Find a place that needs you every month instead of six places needing you twice a year.

Make a portable file of all the information required for credentialing, such as your curriculum vitae, medical licenses, DEA license, board certification, etc. Carry this file with you everywhere you go. Then, if an organization contacts you needing something updated, you will have it with you. You could also do this electronically by scanning all your important documents into one file on your laptop computer and backing it up in the cloud. Then if an organization needed something, it is only a few mouse clicks away. Be sure you update your files immediately when new information arrives, such as your new ACLS card.

ALWAYS ON CALL WHEN WORKING

You might feel uneasy about committing to taking call every day for a week, which is 168 straight hours. Almost all small hospitals have call rotations of seven days in a row for specialists. In a large hospital, with several admits or consults each day, you could not tolerate a multiday call rotation. But smaller rural hospitals have a different volume level.

During my three-year stint of working in CAHs, I averaged 0.9 new patients a day. Many times I have gone three days in a row without a single page. With no clinic responsibilities and less than one new patient a day, the consecutive call days were quite tolerable. It was rare to have back-to-back days of poor sleep. I found I could go ahead and live an almost normal life on call at a CAH, whereas in the larger hospital, I could do nothing beyond surgery on my call day. The small hospital only required a couple of hours a day of my time. The rest of the day was free to write books, read novels, write articles, read journals, take walks with my wife, and enjoy a slower lifestyle than I had experienced for the previous twenty years. Being on call for seven days in a row at a CAH is not usually a problem for a specialist. My final week of call was filled with only three surgeries: a cholecystectomy, a right colon resection, and an appendectomy. Not bad for a full week's pay. Primary care doctors will tend to have shift work in this setting and not be on call 24/7.

NOT EVERYONE USES THE SAME EHR

Each time you work in another hospital, you will need to learn their electronic health records system. You may become familiar with several systems, and fortunately there are not that many to learn. Many hospitals use the same system—Epic being the most common. They vary widely in complexity. A complex system may require fourteen hours of classroom training, and you will still need someone's assistance, while a simpler system might only require 30 minutes of training and you will be good to go. If you are lucky, they will be using a system you are already familiar with. If not, learning a second system is not as bad as it sounds. If you have ever learned any foreign languages, you know that learning a second and third new language is easier than learning the first one.

With the slower pace, you have plenty of time to see your patients and complete the computer charting without any time pressure. Imagine if you only had one patient to see today. You could spend as much time with the patient as you needed and still be able to get the computer chart work done. Both you and the patient would be very happy with that time schedule. The hospital will often supply someone to sit with you at first to help you along. It's in their best interest to help you learn to use their EHR well, since it is how they get paid.

SOME OF YOUR SKILLS WILL DECLINE

As your volume decreases, your proficiency will also decrease. You will not be as fast as you once were, but you won't need to be. Some diagnoses you may no longer see. For me, I saw plenty of appendicitis, bowel obstructions, cholecystitis, and incarcerated hernias. I did not see any thyroids, breasts, Nissen fundoplications, or skin lesions. It's not that I couldn't still do these cases after having done so many over the years, but they were not the cases coming through the emergency department, so the elective cases became nonexistent. Some of those cases may be your favorites and you might miss doing them. That is the trade-off for a lighter work schedule. Since you will generally be seeing the same few cases, even though your numbers go down, you will stay proficient at what you are doing.

Sending away cases you would normally do may be hard on your ego. In a larger hospital setting, there may be no limitations to the care provided. In a smaller hospital where manpower and subspecialty limitations exist, you will need to send away cases you would normally be comfortable handling. If the facility doesn't have inpatient dialysis, cardiology, endoscopy, or invasive radiology, the patients who might need these things will not be staying under your care.

YOU MAY BE LIVING IN A HOTEL

At first this may be exciting. Being in a hotel will feel like you are on a vacation, a nice change of pace. After a while though, the novelty may wear off. Do what you can to make it more like home. Bring along things from home like your exercise CDs, laptop computers, projects, kitchen appliances, and dishes. If you will be going back to a location regularly—for, say, a week every month—rent an apartment and keep your belongings there so you don't have to pack every time. The hospital may be willing to compensate you for a permanent place to live instead of a hotel, in exchange for coming every month to help. The cost to them is not that different. They get a consistent doctor who doesn't need retraining and you get consistent housing. A win-win deal.

HELPFUL TIPS FOR THE LOCUM TENENS LIFE

MALPRACTICE INSURANCE

You should end your personal malpractice insurance coverage. (Be aware, as I discuss elsewhere in this book, of your malpractice tail cost.) You will then have each facility provide malpractice coverage while you work for them. If you are working for a locum tenens company, they will take care of this and you will not need to worry about a tail. If you contract with a nearby facility on your own, be sure they will be responsible for the tail coverage. If they are self-insured, be sure you will be covered for anything that happens while you work for them, no matter when the suit is filed. Bottom line: Make sure you are covered at **their** expense for any claims made in relation to your work, no matter when the claims are made.

PAPERWORK

Carry a file of all your credentialing information with you, both in paper and electronic forms.

Keep the number of locations low to reduce paperwork and relearning.

MAKING IT MORE LIKE HOME

Set up a box of items to bring that will make life away seem more like home.

Bring projects with you so you always have something to do (crafts, hobbies, reading . . .).

Keep up an exercise routine and ask for a hotel with exercise facilities.

Find a local place of worship to attend while you are in town.

If you plan to frequent the same place, get more permanent housing (condo or apartment) and become part of the community.

Be sure you have Internet connections where you stay.

Make a box of kitchen utensils you like to use.

Bring books/magazines/journals to read.

Don't forget laptop accessories like cables, portable printer, and extra paper.

COST CUTTING

Get hotels with a refrigerator and microwave so you can make your own meals.

Make freezer meals, bring food with you, and eat like you are at home.

Try not to eat out all the time.

Bring your own movies and entertainment or use Netflix or something similar on your computer.

MAKING IT FUN

Act like you are on vacation and enjoy the town where you are working.

Work in places you'd like to visit.

Make some friends at the new site, especially if you will be returning. You can expedite this by having dinner with some of the other doctors' families, joining a gym, attending worship activities . . .

Bring your spouse if possible or at least ask your family to visit while you are there.

Bring your bikes, golf clubs, tennis rackets, or equipment for other fun pastimes.

If you are a musician, bring your instrument.

TIME-SAVERS AND CONVENIENCES

Stay packed. Don't unpack when you get home (OK, maybe just the dirty clothes); keep everything ready to put back in the car.

Keep a list of things you need to take so you don't forget things, with a copy in your suitcase.

A George Foreman grill is a great item to cook with when traveling.

Find housing close enough to walk to the hospital so your spouse can use the car.

If possible, drive to your assignment so you can take more stuff (not just a suitcase).

When possible, choose hospitals using the EHR system you already know.

FINAL THOUGHTS ON WORKING PART TIME IN CAHS

Working in this kind of setting can be very rewarding. It provides a transition into retirement. Most doctors are type A personalities, and going from a full workload to no work at all may be quite a shock. Likewise, it will be very important to have a plan for how you will utilize the free time you create by working part time so you never feel like you are twiddling your thumbs. Cutting back to part time is a good way to ease into the life of leisure. It took two years of working part time before I was finally feeling like I could stop practicing medicine and not miss it. It took me that long to wind down from a busy twenty-year career.

If all doctors would do a two-to-three-year period of working part time in a rural area within a few hours' drive of their home, we could make a real dent in the shortage of doctors in rural America. It is such a simple idea and could make such a huge impact. Doctors could slow down gradually. Rural hospitals could get a boost in workforce. Doctors could supplement their retirement income. If your savings are not quite enough to stop working completely, the part-time income could be the bridge you need. The advantages of such a program go on and on. You spent so many years honing your skills, it would be a shame to just toss them out. Find a way to get some extra mileage out of them while not working so hard.

There is a real need for doctors who have a wealth of experience. Many of the locum tenens pool of doctors are fresh out of training, or have never held a job for more than a year. If you were looking for someone to cover your practice for a couple of weeks while you were on vacation, would you prefer to hire someone with six months' experience or twenty years' experience? You will find your skills and experience are in high demand. To a rural hospital, finding a doctor who was in a stable situation for many years and wants to cut back is like finding a pot of gold at the end of the rainbow.

Chapter 6

THE FINANCIAL PHASES
OF YOUR LIFE

Most doctors believe they will be paid a high income for their work. For many of you, it leads to an assumption that you will not need to worry about what you do with your money, as more will be coming in soon. This thought process can cause you to ignore investing for the future, as the future is expected to take care of itself. This casual attitude can also lead to a life of overspending and debt accumulation. This is why a spending plan is important. It keeps you grounded with the understanding that your funds are indeed limited and you should be using them wisely.

Your spending plan evolves throughout your life in three phases: the learning years (training), the earning years (working), and the burning years (retirement). Understanding this evolution will help you manage your resources effectively and plan for a comfortable retirement.

LEARNING YEARS

During medical school and residency, financially you are just trying to keep your head above water. At first, while still in school, you usually borrow money to live on and pay tuition. Then when you get that first paying job as a resident, you can finally stop borrowing money to eat. You begin the process of juggling your debt and postponing payments until your income increases as an attending physician.

Saving for retirement during the learning years is most likely not on your radar yet—but saving some retirement money is possible, if you are thinking about it. Some residency programs even offer a retirement program. I was one of those residents who considered it and was able to put money into my retirement plan, starting in my internship year. That early start made a difference in my future retirement date.

EARNING YEARS

When you finally become an attending, you usually don't start making a meaningful dent in your student loans right away— you live it up a little first, after doing without for so long during the learning years. Many doctors go farther into debt by taking vacations, buying a house, replacing cars, and purchasing other toys after all those years of deprivation. However, if you commit to paying down your loans before taking on significant new debt, you can avoid paying thousands of dollars in interest.

Somewhere during this period, you may come to realize you need to begin saving for retirement. Depending on how early you figure this out and how deeply you are in debt, you may have plenty of time to accumulate your desired retirement funds. On the other hand, if you begin to think about your retirement later in life you may be in panic mode, worrying you will not be able to save enough in time to retire when you want to.

Somewhere in mid-career, your debt probably levels off when you realize it is causing some issues. As you near retirement, you begin to contemplate that debt and how it will affect you in retirement. At some point, you might calculate what amount of savings you will need to retire. You also begin planning for your children's college education, so they will hopefully start their careers with less debt than you did.

During this phase of life, my hope is that you realize debt is limiting your options and your future and begin setting up a spending plan to pay it off before entering the next phase— the burning years. That plan should include setting a *finish line* for yourself—that is, determining how much money you need in passive income, savings, and investments to sustain your retirement.

THE BURNING YEARS

Now the fun begins. You finished funding your children's education. You completed the earning years, crossed your finish line, and want to relax, travel, and enjoy your remaining days. It is important, as you transition into this phase, that you focus on your new spending patterns in retirement. Since you are no longer earning money, what you have saved will need to last for the rest of your life as well as your spouse's life.

WHAT'S DIFFERENT ABOUT RETIREMENT

Debt is a real concern in the burning years. With no earning power, taking on a debt obligation becomes dangerous. Early on, you may feel it is no big deal, since you could just go back to work. As the years go by, there will come a time when going back to work, at least in your prior profession, will not be an option. You must plan carefully during this phase.

I recommend strongly that you don't borrow any money in this phase of your life. You cannot afford to be on the paying end of interest during the burning years (retirement). You need to be accumulating and living on interest, not worrying about paying off debt.

THE CRUCIAL IMPORTANCE OF A SPENDING PLAN

Having a good spending plan (budget) is always important to your wealth, but it is critical in this phase when replacing your savings is not going to be possible. Many people mistakenly think since they are no longer earning any money, they don't need a budget.

Most people, and perhaps especially doctors, find excuses at every stage of life to avoid making a spending plan. Students don't think they have enough *money* to budget. Residents don't think they have enough *time* to budget. Attendings have such a high income they don't think they *need* to budget. And when they retire, they come full circle back to not earning any money so they *still* don't think they need a budget.

Don't fall into this trap. If you haven't been keeping a budget and carefully watching where your money goes before now, then don't delay its implementation. You need a good spending plan. You can download a spending plan form from my website, DrCorySFawcett.com. Be sure to use the right plan to match the phase of your financial life—learning, earning, or burning. My book *The Doctors Guide to Eliminating Debt* covers the topic of developing a spending plan in depth, so I won't repeat it here.

There are a few things that are different about your spending plan during the burning years, so let's cover those.

DETERMINE YOUR INCOME

Hopefully, you will have money sitting in retirement plans at this stage. Figuring out how to utilize this money is kind of like walking across a stream on the rocks and trying to not get wet. If you do anything wrong, you will pay a penalty. It was easy when you were earning money—you had paychecks and W2 forms to tell you what you earn. Now, *you* determine what your income will be by deciding how much money to take out of your investment and retirement accounts, while staying within the government's tax guidelines. And there's some strategy to keep in mind when you make those decisions.

Since money protected from taxes compounds most efficiently, you should work to spend it last. Start using the money outside of your retirement plans and let the retirement accounts continue to grow tax-free as long as possible. For every million dollars you have saved in your retirement plans, you will earn an extra $80,000 tax-free for every year you can avoid tapping into this source, if your investments are growing at 8%. If you have already begun taking Social Security, you will need less of your savings to meet your expenses. Any passive income, like rental return, will also reduce the amount you need to withdraw.

During the earning years, income was fixed and expenses were variable; now it is somewhat reversed. With that in mind, one approach you might take in this phase is to determine the expenses first, which may be the more fixed portion of your spending plan, and that will determine how much income to take from your retirement plan and other investments.

If your initial budget does not require you to use more than 4% of your savings, as I discuss below, then you have room to expand your spending if you wish. You can spend more money to get to 4% or you can take less money, which will leave a larger inheritance. If you have room to increase your withdrawal rate, you can travel a little more or on a bigger budget—for instance, maybe you can fly first class. Someone once told me this about flying:

Always fly first class. If you don't, your son-in-law will.

However, be careful about expanding your expenses to meet your income. So many people do this—just because you have the money doesn't mean you need to spend it. Think about balance and stay within a careful spending plan.

MINIMUM DISTRIBUTIONS

If your retirement accounts have deferred taxes, like a 401(k) or a traditional IRA, the government will not allow you to defer paying taxes forever. When you reach age 70½, you must start taking out a minimum distribution and paying the deferred taxes. This rule doesn't apply to Roth instruments, as no tax will ever be owed on them, so the government doesn't care when you withdraw that money during your lifetime.

Take special note of periodic large expenses and prepare to utilize these required minimum distributions to cover them. Don't let these expenses come as a surprise and catch you without enough cash, tempting you to borrow money during your retirement. You should be thinking about this ahead of time and planning for such a purchase—for example, a car replacement. On or before December 31, you might need to take a required minimum distribution for the year. That would be a good time to replace your car. You could pay cash for the new one using the extra money you must take out of your retirement plan, which will save you the interest costs of a car loan.

You will need to keep an eye on your required minimum distributions so you are not hit with penalties. These are the slippery rocks in the stream. Don't try figuring this out yourself. Use your accountant for this calculation, so you increase the chance of getting it right and don't fall into the stream and get wet. These calculations are based on your life expectancy and therefore change every year.

RATE OF WITHDRAWAL

Much talk and many calculations go into finding the optimum rate for spending down your retirement money without running out. A good rule of thumb is to limit your rate of withdrawal to 4% of your portfolio. This will maximize your spending while increasing the chance your savings will last your entire lifetime. If you draw no more than 4% of your money out of your retirement accounts each year, you will likely have plenty of money for the rest of your life. The more you exceed this, the more likely you will outlive your savings.

With investment returns and interest being lower than average right now (as of this book's publication), some people are beginning to talk about lowering this recommendation to 3%. Consider the state of your overall health as well. If you are in poor health, you can withdraw money at a faster rate, since you will likely have a shorter-than-average life span. If you are in great health and your chances of having a long life are good, then it is best not to exceed a 4% withdrawal rate. It is the safe play.

EARLY DISTRIBUTIONS

Another slippery rock in the stream is the early distribution penalty. If you are not yet 59½, you can incur tax penalties if you do not handle the withdrawals from your tax-deferred retirement accounts exactly right. Doing it right involves using the exceptions listed under IRS rule 72(t). This rule will allow you to begin withdrawing money from your retirement accounts before age 59½ without paying any penalties, *provided* you take the money in "substantially equal periodic payments" (SEPPs). These payments will be based on a calculation of your life expectancy and must continue for five years or until you reach age 59½, whichever is longer. After age 59½, and before age 70½, you will be able to withdraw the money however you wish without incurring any penalties.

Some will argue to take the money out of your Roth IRA first, before any account that will tax the withdrawal, thus postponing your tax bill. The longer you postpone paying income taxes, the better. Others argue the opposite, to take the money subject to taxes out first while the account is smaller and let the Roth continue to grow so withdrawals from the larger account will be tax-free. Hopefully you have enough money that these nuances won't matter. Ask your accountant to help you figure out which method will be best for you.

HEALTH SAVINGS ACCOUNT (HSA)

Now is the time to begin using your HSA account, if you have one. I will discuss this account more in depth in the chapter on passive income, but essentially the account is like an IRA account for medical expenses and is available to those with a high-deductible health insurance policy. Before retirement, you should only make deposits and never withdrawals from this account and let it grow for maximum tax advantage. In retirement, when you are dependent on your savings to pay the bills, you should begin using your HSA to pay for qualified medical expenses. Every time you have a medical bill, co-pay, prescription, or medical insurance premium to pay, do it with the money from this account. Money from your HSA used for those purposes will not be taxed. If you do need to use this money for something other than health expenses, you can use it but you will pay a 20% tax penalty on the money you withdraw.

REBALANCING INVESTMENTS

In retirement, rebalancing your investments will be more important than ever. You should have a good portion of your investments in income production instruments like bonds and money market accounts, as opposed to all stocks. When you need to take the money out to spend it, you don't want to be cashing in stocks or mutual funds invested in stocks. The stock market is too volatile. You cannot take the risk that when you need to make a required distribution, the market is down and you are forced to sell stocks at a loss.

Establish a portion of your investments to be in nonvolatile, stable investments. If your stock proportion is getting too high, sell some of your winners in an up market and convert them to cash-type investments. Then you are always selling stock when you want, and are never forced to sell at a bad time. Always use these cash instruments when you take money out of your retirement plan.

You may not feel you have the time or the knowledge to handle your own investments. If that is your situation, then you need a good financial advisor who is doing this for you. You should be paying them for their time and advice—not based on your portfolio size or per trade they make. Explain to your advisor the strategy you wish to use and be sure your accounts are balanced in the way most suited to you at this stage in your life.

Everyone has a theory for what percentage of your investments should be in stocks/bonds/cash. A lot has to do with your personal risk tolerance. Some who do not ever want to lose any principal will feel 0% stock is the right amount. Others who will feel bad if they miss out on a great run on the stock market want to be 100% invested in stock. A reasonable compromise might be 60% stock, 20% bonds, and 20% cash when you are retired and pulling money out. There are many theories, but you should settle in on a ratio that will allow you to sleep well at night.

SUPPLEMENTAL HEALTH INSURANCE AND THE RIGHT INSURANCE

Consider getting a supplemental insurance policy (Medigap) in addition to Medicare, to pay the difference between what you owe for medical care and what Medicare will pay. They are not very expensive policies but they are much more complicated to choose from than one would expect. However, if you have a very good stockpile of money—more than you need—this insurance may not be worth it to you. Look it over closely with your accountant. **Remember, insurance is not there to make**

you money—it is there to cover an unexpected loss that you can't afford to finance yourself.

Now is the time to be sure you have dropped all the insurance premium bills you don't need. You will not need disability insurance anymore since you no longer *earn* a living and your family is no longer in need of covering a loss of your ability to produce an income from your labor. You will not need life insurance anymore since your family is now financially secure and no longer in need of additional money in the event of your death and inability to *earn* an income—with one exception.

If you have an asset that will be inherited which comes with a tax burden your heirs can't pay otherwise, you might still need life insurance. This might include a valuable business or farm you own. If your heirs will be inheriting a $10 million piece of property and must pay the inheritance taxes and you don't have enough cash to cover that, then life insurance may make sense, if the premium is still affordable. You will be covering an expense with the life insurance policy that your heirs otherwise can't afford to shoulder.

WHAT ABOUT THE LATE BLOOMER?

Not everyone started saving for retirement the moment they started earning an income. Many doctors never even think about retirement savings until late in their career. Then as retirement nears, they realize they have nothing saved for the future. How do they go about saving enough for retirement? The answer is the same as wanting a shade tree in the yard. Start now, as the old saying goes.

The best time to plant a tree is twenty years ago. The second-best time is now.

Don't cry over spilt milk is another concept that comes into play here. It doesn't matter if you missed out on many years of compound interest, so stop dwelling on it. What matters is how many more years you will miss out on if you don't start today. Now is when you realized the problem, so now is the time to take action. And if you want a good retirement, you will probably need to take drastic action. You do have choices:

✓ You can work until you die.

✓ You can plan on an extreme lifestyle change when you convert to living only on Social Security payments.

✓ You can make some big changes in your lifestyle now so you can start making large payments to your retirement accounts to have a decent lifestyle in retirement.

You do have more options than you realize, especially when you come to the conclusion that the lifestyle you live now was your choice, and you are free to choose a different, less expensive one. Many come to this realization and feel there is nothing they can cut from their current spending to increase their savings rate. Almost universally, these doctors do not live with a spending plan and don't actually know where they spend their money. Which in turn means they don't know where they could save money either. When getting down to brass tacks, I have found the following in some of these doctors' spending patterns, all of which were considered necessities:

- ✓ They own a home worth $1.7 million, with an average home price in their area of $220,000. Their current mortgage exceeds $800,000.
- ✓ They just bought two new cars, adding $120,000 of new debt.
- ✓ Their kids are in a private high school that charges a tuition greater than most medical schools charge.
- ✓ They still owe more than $500,000 on their yacht.
- ✓ They traveled to eight foreign countries last year, as well as several places in the US.
- ✓ They have a maid, nanny, cook, and gardener.

Most people would think these doctors have room to make cuts in their budget. But they felt these items were necessities and they could not live without them. What items are in your spending plan that you think you can't live without? Try this test. Pretend you just had a major health issue and your ability to practice was cut in half. You can still practice, but your income will take a 50% cut. What items will you be dropping in this scenario?

When people first approach this exercise, they still don't see what they can cut. They have grown so accustomed to their lifestyle, they don't see downsizing as possible. Many other people live fine on half of this income—even a quarter of this income is a good salary for most of America.

Here are some practical examples of how to scale back your spending to free up money for retirement savings:

✓ The doctor who had the $1.7 million house with $800,000 remaining on his mortgage is paying $5,300 a month in principal and interest on his loan. If he were to sell the house and buy a $600,000 house with cash (nearly three times the cost of the local average house), he would still live in a very nice house and would pocket about $200,000. He would eliminate a $5,300 monthly payment. If he then put the cash and the monthly payments into savings and invested it, getting a 6% return in the market for the next fifteen years, the nest egg would exceed $2 million. This would provide an $80,000 annual income for the rest of his life, if he withdraws 4% per year. If he was 50 years old when he realized this, he would be retiring at 65 with a much better outlook financially. That doesn't count the money saved from the lower expenses generated by the less expensive house.

✓ A similar effect is generated by swapping out the yacht mentioned above for a $100,000 pleasure boat. You can still enjoy the time on the water, but the smaller boat allows room for making retirement plan deposits.

✓ Take your vacations at less expensive destinations and save the difference.

✓ Cash out a very expensive universal life insurance policy and buy an appropriate term policy and save the difference.

✓ You might need to delay your retirement a few more years to allow catch-up time.

The list could go on and on with ways to decrease your monthly expenses and put that money toward your future life—the one in which you no longer are working for an income. You can find suggestions on saving money and cutting costs all over the Internet. Look closely at what you spend now, and make some difficult decisions that will improve your future. You are in control of this. You make the spending decisions; set up a good spending plan and begin proactively determining where your money will go and stop spending reactively. This may be an area to seek outside, unbiased help. I offer one-on-one coaching and can be contacted through my website at DrCorySFawcett.com. You might also be able to get this from your accountant or financial advisor. Your future self will be very happy you did this. Start today.

Chapter 7

PREPARING FOR FULL RETIREMENT

If your decision is to take the plunge and fully retire, rather than make a change to something else or modify your practice, then some preparation is in order. Even if you have decided on a career change for now, there will come a time when you will eventually stop working and fully retire. At that point, you will commit to living on your savings, retirement funds, passive income, and possibly Social Security payments.

Before taking that leap, be sure you have all your ducks in a row. Although you may be forced into this step suddenly, like my doctor friend who had an unexpected stroke, most doctors will make this move in a controlled fashion.

Where is the finish line?

In *The Doctors Guide to Eliminating Debt*, I introduced the notion of a *finish line*—that is, the goal you set to reach financial independence. It is not desirable or prudent to go on collecting wealth forever; you need to establish a finish line. Once you cross that line, you have accumulated enough wealth to take care of your needs for the rest of your life. Continuing to accumulate after crossing the finish line is a waste of resources. Instead of stockpiling, at that point you can use your time, energy, and income to better the world, help other family members, and have fun.

Just imagine what it would be like to begin running a marathon without being told the location of the finish line. Which direction do you run? How far do you need to run? What pace do you set to finish and still be standing? When will you know it is time to stop? How will you know if you have won the race?

Yet many people treat retirement savings in this manner—and they will never know when the race is over and will spend their entire lives racing.

You must know your starting point and ending point in order to run an effective race.

My finish line had two components. The first component was a desired amount of annual passive income outside of my retirement plans that could fully cover my living expenses. The second component was a target total value for my retirement savings, which could also cover my living expenses by withdrawing 4% per year. These two together created a retirement plan and a backup plan that was my safety net, in case I calculated wrong or something happened to one of the two components.

You will need to establish a finish line of your own. Let's go over some of the things you need to be thinking about as you establish and approach your finish line.

DON'T CARRY DEBT INTO RETIREMENT

It is unwise to plan on carrying debt into your retirement years. Many advisors will tell you differently, but I wholeheartedly disagree with them. If an accountant or financial management professional tells you this, ask them if they know this firsthand, from clients who have carried debt into their retirement and are happy about the decision, or is this advice just a theory. Debt not only significantly increases the amount of money you must save for retirement, it adds stress and worry to your life.

Beware of Alzheimer's Debtmentia and Debtabetic Neuropathy.

Any obligation to pay someone money psychologically weighs you down, especially if you are no longer earning money. Many doctors do not appreciate the burden debt places on their shoulders. I certainly didn't. It was only after I paid off my final debt and felt the weight lifted from me, that I realized it had been there all along. I had been in debt for so long, I no longer realized the effect it had on me. I had Alzheimer's Debtmentia, a condition characterized by forgetting what it was like to be debt-free. Another thing I suffered from was Debtabetic Neuropathy, I had become numb to the effects of debt. Retirement is supposed to be a time of peace and tranquility. Debt is an obstacle in attaining that relaxed state.

Planning to carry debt into retirement also substantially increases the amount of money you must save to be ready for retirement and may delay your retirement date by years. The most common debt people want to carry into retirement is their home mortgage, usually because they perceive it to be too hard to pay off. That is not the case. It is not difficult to eliminate your mortgage before you retire, but it must be one of your goals in order for it to happen.

Debt has a lot of downsides, and they become critical during retirement. I was recently coaching a couple who lived in a very expensive home. They were nearing the age where retirement was a consideration, and they were worried they would not have enough money to retire. They had recently refinanced their $800,000 mortgage for another thirty years. Their mortgage payments were almost $60,000 a year. In addition, the upkeep of the house and property, which required hired hands, amounted to another $60,000 a year.

If they were to retire with this mortgage as part of their expenses, they would need an extra $60,000 annual net income—or $100,000 per year gross income—from their retirement plan to cover the payments, not counting the upkeep. They would need an additional $2.5 million in their retirement account (to withdraw 4% a year to get the $100,000 gross retirement income) in order to pay the $40,000 in taxes and net the $60,000 needed to make the mortgage payments. They would need a little less if the retirement funds were in Roth products that would not be taxed.

This simple way of showing the financial impact of that one decision demonstrates the need to save an extra $2.5 million in their retirement plan in order to make the payments on an $800,000 loan, which doesn't make sense.

A more logical solution would be to sell their very expensive house, which was valued at more than double the mortgage, buy a less expensive but very nice house with the cash from the sale, and reduce their needed retirement savings by $2.5 million.

It takes a long time to save up $2.5 million. Carrying that debt into retirement would force him to work many more years. The more they thought about it, the more they realized the house was holding them back. He wanted to retire sooner—$2.5 million sooner. It is a very expensive and often impractical proposition to carry debt into your retirement.

Another doctor came to me, thinking he needed to work for five more years to have enough saved for retirement. He also still owed money on his home. I looked over his finances and realized if he used some of his savings to pay off the house, he already had enough to retire. He was only working the next five years so he could save enough money to cover the house payments. Again, maintaining the debt made no sense. He retired one month after our conversation.

Debt may cause you to work more years, longer hours, or more days per week and is a burden you don't need when you retire. It is imperative to pay off all debt before you quit producing an income. Of course, I recommend you pay it all off much earlier than that—but even if you don't or can't do that, don't plan on retiring with debt hanging around your neck. Otherwise, your retirement may not be as soon or as peaceful as you had in mind.

ESTABLISH AN ACCURATE SPENDING PLAN

You will need an accurate estimate of what it takes to live the life you want during your retirement years. You may be working so furiously on the treadmill of production that you find yourself constantly in a crisis mode of spending. Whatever yells the loudest is what gets the money. You may have never taken the time to determine your true financial needs. Instead, you take the easy way out and mistakenly assume you will be living on 80% of your preretirement income, as you so often read. You may want to do some neat stuff when you retire, such as travel. Consequently, once you are retired, you might spend more money than when you were working.

Many doctors don't ever make a spending plan—also known as a budget—and without one, it is almost impossible to establish a finish line. Long before you retire, you should determine what your life will look like. Traveling takes money, and depending on the style you like to travel in, it could be a lot of money. You need to know exactly what it will take for you to reach your retirement dreams before you make the jump.

Not having a spending plan makes the finish line nebulous. Having a well-thought-out spending plan will give you confidence as you begin this great journey. Don't skip this step. It might be the single most important part of planning your retirement. Visit my website DrCorySFawcett.com for a downloadable spending plan form, or see my step-by-step description of how to develop a spending plan in *The Doctors Guide to Eliminating Debt*.

TWO BIG EXPENSES YOU WON'T NEED IN RETIREMENT

Two things you can drop from your spending plan in retirement are life insurance and disability insurance. Once you have enough wealth accumulated to take care of your family for the rest of their dependent years, you will no longer need these insurance plans. They will have fulfilled their purpose of keeping your family safe and protected in your early earning years, in the event you could no longer provide an adequate income.

Life insurance

Many doctors feel an intense need to keep their life insurance in place. They either can't let go of something they have had for so long, like a comfort blanket, or they want to leave a larger inheritance for their kids. Don't fall into that trap. You should not be working and earning money to make a bigger nest egg for your kids. Their nest egg is their own responsibility to accumulate. You have a big enough task to build a nest egg for you and your spouse and in doing so, you will leave behind a significant inheritance.

Trying to make money with life insurance is not a good idea. You don't want to be worth more dead than alive. Use it for what it was intended—to insure the financial fitness of your family if you are no longer there to do so yourself. Once you have crossed the finish line, that goal is met and your family is taken care of. At that point you are self-insured, so don't waste any more money on insurance you don't need. Your children should not be counting on money from you for their retirement. Encourage them to build their own life and establish their own finish line.

Disability insurance

Disability insurance is another expense you can drop. Disability policies pay you until you are able to collect full Social Security benefits, which begin between ages 65 and 67, depending on your birth year. The closer you are to your full Social Security benefits age, the less value disability insurance has for you. In other words, each year the policy loses value since it will pay for your disability for one less year. Drop this as soon as you cross the finish line. You can find better uses for those premiums.

NEW EXPENSES IN RETIREMENT

Health insurance

You will need to replace your office or employee health insurance policy with a personal one. Check into the COBRA (Consolidated Omnibus Budget Reconciliation Act) laws and see how the premiums compare in price to purchasing a new individual plan. It may be beneficial to stay on your current policy for a while. If it is cheaper than one you can get on your own, keep it as long as possible.

I gained a new appreciation for what my patients go through when I had to get my own health insurance policy. Until then, whatever the office had, I had. There are so many options. Once you decide on one company, you will then have several plans to choose from, with multiple complicated options. It's a wonder I ended up with any insurance at all. But getting coverage is critical. You don't want to get caught without health insurance. You may even know someone without health insurance who was forced into bankruptcy due to an unexpected hospital bill. Since you should have a good nest egg by now, a high-deductible plan should work out fine and save some money on premiums if you haven't reached Medicare age yet.

Don't forget about Medicare

Many doctors have spent their lives griping about the low payments Medicare provides for caring for their patients. Now you will need to wrestle with this issue from the other side of the fence. Once you are a Medicare patient, you will appreciate the doctor who will accept assignment. The shoe is on the other foot.

Medicare, like every other government program, is much more complicated than it needs to be. Work very hard to not miss their deadlines. When you turn 65, you can sign up for Medicare. You have a small window to get signed up—three months before and after your 65th birthday is the penalty-free period, and coverage will start the first day of your birthday month. If you miss this window, you will pay extra for signing up late. Also if you miss this window, you can only sign up between January 1 and March 31 of each year, and your coverage will begin the following July 1. Don't miss the age 65 window.

Medicare does not cover all your medical bills. You will be responsible for a portion of the expenses. That is why you should also consider a supplemental insurance plan, also known as

Medigap policies, which "fill in the gaps," the portion of your medical bills that Medicare does not cover. You need to purchase a Medigap coverage plan during the open enrollment period, which lasts for six months and begins the first day of the month after you turn 65 and are enrolled in Medicare part B. After that period, they can deny you coverage or charge you a larger fee. So if you want this coverage, don't miss the window.

Long-term care insurance

One type of insurance you should probably **not** have at this point is long-term care. For the average American who has very little in savings, there may be a benefit for this type of insurance. For the average high-income earner, you should have plenty of savings to cover long-term care needs. If you have crossed the finish line, you are unlikely to need long-term care insurance. If you need long-term care, you won't be traveling or spending other money and are not likely to need your money for very much longer. Healthy people tend to live a lot longer than those who need a long-term care facility. So for high-income individuals who are near the finish line, this insurance is usually not needed—for the same reason you no longer need life insurance, because you are essentially self-insured. In your younger years, when you have a low net worth, it may be of benefit.

I witnessed my grandparents' long-term care needs firsthand and their experiences make good examples. Both of my grandfathers died of cancer fairly quickly at an earlier age and would not have benefitted from this insurance. Both my grandmothers became frail at a much later age and eventually needed to live in memory care centers, at which time this insurance would have come into play.

Each of my grandmothers had to pay $4,500 per month for a memory care facility. Once they reached the point of needing long-term care, they were nearing the end of their lives. One needed this service for eight months before she passed away, for a total cost of $36,000 plus some start-up fees. The other was in a long-term care facility for two and a half years before her death. She needed a total of $135,000 plus start-up fees to cover her care. For each of them, the proceeds from selling their home, which they no longer needed, more than covered their long-term care needs without even dipping into their savings.

You should consider long-term care in the same way you think about life insurance. Early in your life, you don't have enough money saved to protect your family from disaster if you die, so you buy life insurance. Later in life, when your savings are substantial enough that your family will be OK financially without you, you don't need life insurance. With long-term care, you are vulnerable early on when you have a small amount in savings. Later, with a large amount saved, you are not vulnerable and don't need the insurance.

Long-term care insurance is usually limited. The policy will likely have either a time limit (i.e., you will be covered for a maximum of three years) or a dollar limit (i.e., you will be covered up to $200,000).

The policy may also have both limits in play. So if you have significantly more than $200,000 in your savings, you have enough money to self-insure your long-term care needs if they arise.

Others make the argument for not wanting to burn through savings to cover this care. But isn't that why you saved it in the first place? You were putting money away to take care of yourself in the future, when you are no longer able to earn a living. Burning through your savings is exactly what you put it there to do and exactly what will happen when you eventually retire.

Every source you find will give a slightly different average time period for long-term care needs, but they are all in the vicinity of three years. One of my grandmothers came close to that average. And the care needs for a nursing home, the most expensive long-term care option, will be in the range of $70,000 a year. Some parts of the country are higher and some are lower. Three years at $70,000 a year is $210,000, and if you have crossed the finish line, you will have significantly more than that.

Most doctors who have been saving money will have a net worth exceeding a million dollars at the time they will need long-term care. It is unlikely you and your spouse will need more care than you have money to cover. Long-term care insurance is a less important consideration for high-income earners, especially those who have crossed the finish line. The groups who benefit from it the most are those with little to no savings. If you are in this group, then it may be a good option, otherwise use your money elsewhere.

Increased travel expenses (or other fun activities)

Many doctors want to travel more when they stop working. If you are one of them, you should increase the amount in the vacation section of your budget. Travel can be expensive and you should do your best to get an accurate estimate for this. Look up a few trips you would like to take and account for the expense. Add another 10% for good measure, as you will likely forget things and underestimate what you will spend while you are having fun at the resort. It's fun to have fun so plan for it.

ESTIMATE YOUR TAXES

Using the numbers from your projected retirement spending plan, you will need to estimate the taxes you will pay on your retirement withdrawals. If you have passive income and Social Security payments coming in, subtract those amounts from your total expenses to estimate the net income amount you will need from your retirement plans to balance your budget. Add in the taxes on those withdrawals, and you have the total you need to remove from your retirement funds each year.

There are many ideas floating around about how much you should be taking out of your retirement plans annually, but most of them are near 4%. If your withdrawals do not exceed 4% of the total amount in the account, there is a good chance you will never outlive your retirement funds. If you take out more, the risk of running out of money begins to climb. If you take out less, you are leaving more money to your heirs and missing a chance to do some fun things you have saved for all these years. Four percent seems to be a happy balance.

When you have established the total amount you need to withdraw from your retirement plans to balance your spending plan, multiply this amount by 25 to establish the total funds you will need in your retirement plan. This figure can be used to help establish your finish line.

DECIDE WHEN TO TAKE SOCIAL SECURITY

This is a controversial topic that I believe has no controversy for the high-income earner. Beginning to take your Social Security payments before your designated full-retirement age—for me that's 67—will result in a lower monthly payment. Waiting until later, such as at age 70, will increase your monthly payments, but you lose out on all the money you could have taken for the prior years—an opportunity cost.

This question is similar to the choice of going to medical school versus starting to work right out of college. If you start work right out of college, you will have a lower income. If you go to medical school and residency, your income will likely be greater, but you don't start it for another seven to twelve years. You will not only miss out on the income all those years, but you will also be paying interest on the money you borrowed to get through school. It is a trade-off that is easier to make when you are young and likely have many years ahead.

When you reach retirement age, your risk of dying in any given year is climbing. So your chances of collecting that higher Social Security payment long enough to surpass the earlier payment drops each year. If you think of this as a linear equation involving the money collected, the breakeven point is around age 79. If you will live beyond that, you are better off waiting until you are 70 to collect Social Security. If you don't believe you will make it to 79, then start collecting at 62. The reality is, you don't know how long you will live.

The chart on the next page shows how my benefits play out by starting Social Security withdrawals at age 62 ($1,868 per month), 67 ($2,818 per month), and 70 ($3,511 per month) according to the information sent to me by the Social Security Administration.

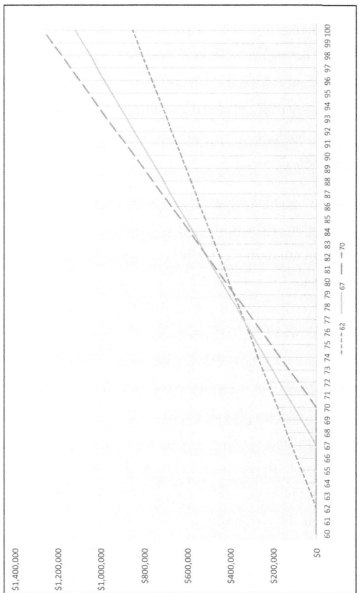

Comparing Social Security payout totals based on age at which you start collecting them.

This is a very popular chart that most doctors should not be using to make their decision. I believe a different chart and way of thinking is in order. I often hear this advice, "If you don't need the money to live on, wait until age 70 and draw the larger number." But if you don't need the money, you could invest it rather than spend it if you were to take it early. That means you should be taking into account the interest accruing on each of the three choices.

If I were to begin taking my $1,868 a month at age 62, and I am living off my retirement funds at that time, I can now leave $1,868 a month in the retirement account and let it continue to grow while I use my Social Security payments to live on. Thus the overall return on my retirement plan will effectively apply to the Social Security payments. With this in mind, the chart takes on a whole new look. This also leaves out the effects of avoiding any taxes the retirement plan money might require to be paid. Older people may not have a Roth alternative available in their plan and will be paying taxes on the withdrawals. Younger people should have a considerable portion in Roth accounts and no taxes enter the equation. So for this example, we leave out the taxes and just look at the effect interest will have on the decision.

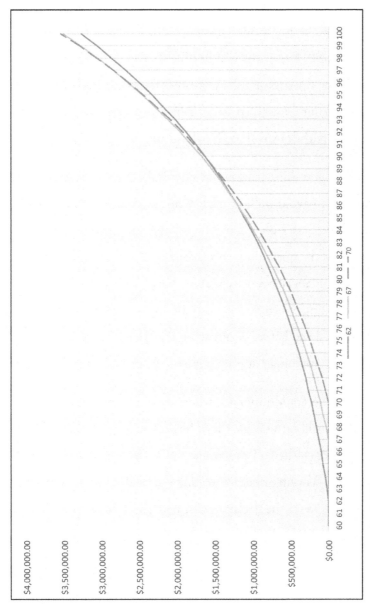

Social Security payout totals that include 6% investment return on those payments.

As you can see, interest accumulation changes everything. At 6% interest, I will be 90 years old before I would do better by waiting to take my money until age 70. Not very many people live to age 90, and most will be able to average better than 6% return over the long haul. At an 8% return or higher, no one has lived long enough to benefit from waiting until age 70 to begin the withdrawal since Noah's time.

So even if you don't need the money, take it as soon as possible and use it to avoid pulling money out of your retirement plans. You will be better off financially for the choice. If you do need the money, the question is moot. The only reason for a doctor to delay taking Social Security is to still be working. There are penalties to taking Social Security payments while you are still working, if you do so before you reach full retirement age. As soon as the penalty no longer applies, take the money and invest it.

This decision could influence where the finish line gets drawn as well. If you still can't decide (don't forget you are choosing between good choices—they all put money in your pocket), then check with your accountant before making the final decision. Whatever you decide, make the decision with your finish line in mind.

BUY YOUR TOYS AND OTHER BIG PURCHASES BEFORE YOU RETIRE

Some of the things you plan to do in retirement will need equipment. For example, if you want to travel across the United States in an RV, you will need the RV. If you want to do woodworking, you will need the tools in your shop. I recommend you buy these toys before you retire and don't include their purchase in your retirement needs. If you expect you will continue to occasionally purchase tools, include an estimate of that expense in your retirement spending plan.

Also, you will be driving cars for a long time in your retirement. If your cars are already old, you might consider replacing them before you quit working. Going into retirement with cars that will last fifteen years is a very good start. When you are developing your retirement spending plan, estimate when you expect to need new vehicles based on the age of your current vehicles at retirement, and include them in the plan. Cars will last a lot longer than you think. As I write this, I own three cars: an eight-year-old Prius, a thirteen-year-old Ford Expedition, and a nineteen-year-old Toyota Avalon. All of them are in great shape and are very reliable, so we have no plans to replace any of them in the near future.

Make sure you will not be adding to your debt with these purchases—plan to save the money first and pay cash for your automobile purchases.

BE SURE YOU ARE PSYCHOLOGICALLY READY TO QUIT WORKING

Medicine is not like most other professions. If you quit for more than a year, it will be hard to return. Those who are credentialing you will be suspect of your skills if you haven't used them for more than a year.

You may not be ready to stop practicing your craft. You need to be sure of your feelings on this. I know when I left my private practice, I was not ready to quit operating. I worked part time in rural hospitals that were less busy and less stressful, but I was still using my skills. It took about two years before I finally felt I could stop practicing medicine and another year to actually stop for good. Your identity is tied to what you do for a living. Ask yourself honestly if you are ready for that change.

If your psyche is tied to being a doctor, you are not ready to retire yet—and you may be sorry if you do, at this point. Many doctors retire and then go back to work again in less than a year. Many have retired several times. They can't seem to make up their minds as to their readiness for retirement. Don't make the mistake of quitting too soon.

COVERING YOUR TAIL

One of the big surprises you might encounter as you approach retirement is paying for a tail (an extended reporting endorsement) on your malpractice insurance. Many doctors do not know about the tail requirements. In a claims-made policy, you are only covered if you have an active insurance policy at the time the patient makes the claim and the incident occurred during the insured period. If your last patient in practice experienced some type of complication, they will usually have between two and three years to sue you, based on the statute of limitations which is different in every state. The range varies from one to ten years and can be even longer if the patient was a baby at the time of the incident.

In order for you to be covered against future claims, if you have claims-made insurance, you need to purchase a tail for your insurance plan when you retire. This will cover any claim made in the future from an act during your insured period. This can cost a lot of money—usually in the neighborhood of twice your annual malpractice insurance premiums.

If you have been slowing down your practice because you are nearing retirement, as you see fewer patients, your premium should be decreasing and so would your tail. I decreased my patient load to be about a half-time practice in the two years before ending my malpractice insurance, and since I was seeing fewer patients, my risk for a malpractice claim was less, and my premiums fell dramatically. With a lower premium, it would correspond to a lower tail. If you go from full-time practice to retired in one day, the tail will be at its maximum. So a good way to lower your tail cost is to cut back your practice for a while before quitting entirely.

Don't get caught by surprise on this. Check your employment contract to see what type of malpractice coverage you have, occurrence or claims-made, and if it is claims-made, figure out who pays for the tail. If you have occurrence coverage, no tail is needed. It will cover you for anything that occurred during your coverage without regard to when you are actually sued.

It is best for you if someone else is responsible for buying the tail. That is something you should have negotiated into your contract when you were hired. If you didn't know about it at the time you signed your contract, make sure you plan for the repercussions now. Get a copy of your insurance and keep it on file. You won't usually have this unless you specifically ask for it. Do this at the time of your hire and every time you change jobs. It may raise eyebrows if you suddenly ask for this information later.

Many private practices will have you pay your own tail, and many employed positions will offer to pay the tail. If you are responsible for the tail, contact your malpractice insurance agent and make sure you know how much it will be. You don't want to get a bill for a $175,000 tail 30 days after you retire—especially if you were on the edge of having enough money for your retirement. If you know you will be buying a tail, start a savings plan to have the money in place before you retire.

Some insurance companies offer a free tail after you have been insured by them for at least ten years. When you end your practice, and have met their conditions, your tail is free. But if you decide later that you made a mistake and want to go back into practice, the new malpractice insurance policy would likely require you to buy a tail next time. Their free tail is often a once-in-a-lifetime deal.

When I started working part time, each new employer was responsible for my tail in our contract. Never take a part-time job requiring you to purchase a tail when you finish.

Don't be tempted to skip buying a tail to save a few bucks. Many contracts require the tail, so skipping it is not an option. Going bare is too risky when you retire. How would your retirement look if you were sued thirteen months later and lost a $2 million judgment? Then you might be forced to go back to work—most retirees could not afford to give up that much and stay in retirement. You wouldn't want to lose your house and cars at a point when you are no longer earning an income. And going back into the practice of medicine after a few years' break may be difficult, if not impossible, to do.

You could consider a nonclinical career at that point if you had to work again. You are still a doctor who has a lot of knowledge and experience and are a commodity on the job market.

MOVING YOUR RETIREMENT MONEY

Your retirement plan will likely be a large sum. You also may have several retirement plans, if you have been with several organizations throughout your career and never rolled any of the money into another account. You could have two 401(k) accounts from two prior employers, a 403(b) from another, and a SEP-IRA from a short stint in solo practice. You also may have an IRA for both you and a spouse. You may wish to do some consolidating.

There is no compelling reason you need to move any of your retirement plan money. It depends on the level of control you want. If the money stays where it is, you may need to make requests to have distributions, which may result in a time delay. If you move it to your own control, you can just withdraw the money. If you are savvy enough to do your own investing, moving the money to an account you control may be desirable and more flexible.

Discuss this with your accountant and with each plan administrator to determine what is best for you. You may not want to bother with it. Just be sure if you do decide to move it, you do not take any of it as a distribution. Have one plan transfer or roll over the money to another and don't let it pass through you. If you have the money in your possession during the move, it will be considered a distribution and you could end up owing taxes on it if you don't make the transfer correctly. Stay out of the loop and you will be fine.

Chapter 8

MAKING YOUR EXIT

Winding down your practice is not an easy task—for your schedule, your psyche, your spouse, your call partners, or your patients. After many years of practice in the same office, you might find it a little hard to let go. You will also miss seeing your office staff and the hospital staff, as well as the other doctors you have been talking with all these years. In my case, I had worked with some of them for twenty years and suddenly I didn't see them anymore. My name was still up on the sign in front of the office for a while, and I had a knot in my stomach the first time I drove down the street and noticed my name missing from the marquee. In addition to these adjustments, there are a lot of little things to take care of as you close down your practice.

TELLING THE WORLD

One of the biggest tasks is to tell your patients. If you are a dentist or a primary care doctor, you may have had some of those patients for many years. You may even have several generations of the family coming to see you. There is some separation anxiety for them as well as for you. You need to give them some time to find a new doctor. If you have partners taking over your patients, you will need to pick a good time to let your patients know of the change. The minimum is 30 days, but if you know further in advance, your patients will appreciate more notice.

Figure out how you will tell them. A personal letter, emails, ads in the paper, signs in your waiting room. Whatever combination of these methods you use, you will need a little lead time to get things ready.

If your office will be closing, you will need to arrange for the patient records transfer to a new doctor. Someone will need to take the responsibility of assuring your patients have access to their records. If your electronic records system is a different program than the accepting doctor uses, something will need to be done about that. It might be easiest to pick a receiving doctor using the same system.

Your staff will also need some lead time, especially if your retirement means the loss of their job. If there are other doctors in the office, no one is likely to lose their job. That will not be the case for everyone. Your loyal staff will want ample time to find a new job and yet not abandon ship before your time is up. That is a tricky timing issue. Offer to give them good letters of recommendation. If they put many years of good service in for you, help them with the transition. If you are an employee of a hospital, staffing changes still might occur when you leave.

Your colleagues need to know what is happening. Those who saw you at meetings will be wondering where you are. Those doctors who refer to you will need to start a new referral pattern. Make some sort of formal announcement to those doctors in your circle, so they are not taken by surprise when they unknowingly refer a patient to you and the patient comes back saying you retired. This also allows you some closure as other doctors will be telling you thanks for your years of service, and those memories will help you when you later have days of missing your work.

If your work involves a hospital or other healthcare facility, they will need to know exactly what day you are dropping your privileges. Depending on your situation and the hospital policies, you could be either dropped from the staff or be changed to an emeritus doctor. You might be on some committees that will need to find a replacement. They will need to cancel your EHR access at a point when you have completed everything and collect your ID badge, if it is used to gain access to secure parts of the hospital. If you use block time at the hospital for something like the operating room or endoscopy suite, they will be giving that time to another doctor. If you are on a rotation for reading tests like EKGs or stress tests, they will need to make other arrangements.

As your date approaches, make a list of all the people you need to inform and establish the method you will use. Then at the appointed time, make each notification and bow out with grace and style.

SELLING YOUR PRACTICE

If you are in private practice, you might wish to sell your practice. This can be problematic. Your retirement date might be determined by when you can sell the practice. The timing may not work out to your liking. When people know you are selling, they may start finding another doctor to see and if the volume drops, your ability to sell goes down, or at least the price does. For this reason, you may not want your patients to know you are selling until after the sale is complete.

Some doctors will not be able to sell their practice, but instead will be liquidating the office. You may have a building to sell, which will take some time but could be a dandy addition to your retirement income. You may decide to rent the building out to someone else. You will have office equipment to dispose of, much of which will have some resale value if you can connect with a buyer. There are sample medications to deal with as well as office supplies. You might consider giving all the supplies away to another doctor to use on a third world mission trip. Others have given supplies to their friends or a local charity, like the Gospel Rescue Mission.

You might even consider selling your practice to the local hospital, if they are buying up practices. This would allow you to become an employee for a short time before stopping practice altogether.

MEDICAL LICENSE

What you do about your license to practice medicine depends on your future plans. This is a very difficult license to obtain, and may be impossible to replace if you give it up. So think two, three, and even four times before giving it up for good. If, on the other hand, you know for certain you will never practice again, paying for the license is a waste of money.

> Make sure you know if you will need your license, if you are considering a career change.

If you are considering changing careers or working part time, make sure you know if you will need your license to do this work. Some nonclinical career options require a medical license and board certification, and some do not.

If you are planning to do charity work or overseas missionary work, many of these organizations you would be working with will require you to have an active license. Some states have a reduced fee license to do charity care. You have a license to practice medicine but cannot charge for your services. Don't make an irreversible mistake at this juncture. Do your research.

How many doctors do you know who made a decision to retire, only to go back to work later? Unforeseen occurrences could drive you to return to practice. A sudden downturn in the stock market that reduces your retirement account so much it may not last the rest of your life is one such reason that worries many retirees. One of the doctors you worked with could have an accident and ask for your help until he recovers. Because you could change your mind and this is a difficult license to get, you should keep your license active for a while after you retire. The small amount you will pay in fees during this time will be cheap insurance. Check with your state licensing agency to be sure you are meeting the requirements to maintain your license. If you have several state licenses, you only need to keep one active.

When you are ready to change your license, you may have some choices as to what you do. Rather than give it up, you may be able to change categories to something like retired, emeritus retired, voluntary charity care, or inactive. Each state has different options and a quick check with your licensing board will give you those options.

At some point, you will give up the license for good. You will need to inform the Drug Enforcement Agency (DEA) of that as well, so they can remove you from their list of narcotics prescribers. Like your medical license, your DEA license will no longer be needed when you fully retire.

MALPRACTICE INSURANCE

What you do about your malpractice insurance is also a very important decision. Once you drop it, if you have a claims-made policy, you will trigger the need to purchase a tail. This is a very expensive move. It is important for you to know if you are responsible for the tail coverage or if your employer is. I mentioned this in the Preparing for Full Retirement chapter because being surprised with a $100,000 insurance bill would be quite a shock, not to mention a big issue for your spending plan. If you have occurrence-type coverage, you will not need to purchase a tail.

If you are responsible for this coverage, you will need to plan for it. You will need to inform your insurance company of your retirement. You can give them a call to get tail cost estimates for your planning. Depending on what you are doing, you may not be buying a tail yet. If you plan to work part time, for instance, inform your malpractice insurance carrier and they will decrease your premiums, saving you money. Your tail will come later and will be cheaper than if you retired from a full-time practice.

ANCILLARY PROFESSIONAL ORGANIZATIONS

Most doctors belong to several organizations. When you retire, your status may not change with some of them, but others will change your status to a different category. You may still want to receive their periodicals, like the *Journal of the American Medical Association*. Some may require a hefty fee to stay involved with the organization, and you will need to decide if it is worth continuing after you are retired. Continuing to pay dues for multiple professional organizations can get quite expensive and will be unnecessary. Figure out which you will keep and which you will drop.

All the organizational memberships you decide to maintain will need a change of address. If you want their information, you don't want it showing up at the old office and getting thrown away after you are gone. Be sure not to forget all the state medical boards you are licensed with. Missing one of these address changes could cost you a late fee on a state license renewal, if your old office mistakes the renewal notice as junk mail. It is not their job to decide what is and isn't junk mail after you are gone. For a few months before you are making your change, start a list of all the mail you get at the office. You can tear out the page of periodicals that lists their contact information and use that to change your address when the time comes.

Board certification organizations will need to know of your practice change and may be able to put you in an emeritus or retired status. Consider board certification as precious as your state medical license, and keep it as long as you can. There will be more open doors to the doctor who is still listed as board-certified than to one who is not.

ADVERTISING AND SOCIAL MEDIA SITES

If you have a professional Internet presence through a website, LinkedIn, or other social media, once your status changes you should update your status and provide new contact information—if you want people to be able to find you. You should also contact the local phone book to remove your practice name and number from the white and yellow pages of both their online and paper versions. If you are employed, remind your employer to do this. I still see lots of online information about retired doctors, myself included, and it is misleading to patients who might be trying to find you, since you took care of them eight years ago and they want to see you again.

Many doctors use social media for their practice. It would be a good idea to take down those sites or somehow inactivate them if you will no longer be using them. Using those sites to let people know you are retired is helpful. If you have been publishing helpful health information on these sites and are going to continue to do so, then keep your contacts active. You may enjoy updating the social media information with changes in the medical field, even though you are retired.

THINK ABOUT WAYS FOR PEOPLE TO FIND YOU

Many doctors have chosen not to have their home phone numbers listed in the white pages of the phone book. You may want to rethink that after retirement. If a long-lost friend wanted to connect with you again and you have no office and are unlisted, they may be out of luck and so will you. With the popularity of cell phones, many have abandoned their landlines completely, and cell phone numbers aren't listed in a directory. Be sure people can find you.

Having social media pages is a good way to stay in touch. A simple Facebook page will allow those looking for you to find you, especially if you move to another city. I have reconnected with old high school friends this way.

OLD MEDICAL BOOKS

This is a very difficult storage problem to deal with. When I left my office and cleaned out all my books, I stacked them in the garage. Two years later, they were still there. The books are mostly too old for use, as medicine changes so rapidly and many of them are from my medical school days. Online information has taken their place. No one else will want these outdated medical books either—yet it was hard for me to throw them away and you may have the same feelings.

Stacks of journals you saved and cut-out articles you have cataloged are all useless at this point and have probably been useless for quite some time anyway. I looked at the books and realized, now that we have UpToDate and many other online resources, I haven't opened most of my textbooks in years. There were maybe a half-dozen books I referred to, yet eight boxes still sit in the garage.

I was finally able to bite the bullet and sorted out half of them for destruction. It was a start, but it's time to get real. Are those books that you will never read again adding any meaning to your life? Wouldn't you rather have the space they are taking up for something that is adding meaning to your life? Bite the bullet and throw them *all* away. If that is too hard, put them on eBay and see if there is a collector or library out there that might want them. Just don't leave them cluttering up your new life.

OFFICE PERKS

Some office benefits may need to be replaced. For example, during your working years you may have had free access to the hospital gym, but now you will need to get a membership to the local private gym or get some gym equipment to use at home.

One aspect of daily work can be harder to replace: the social interactions. You will not be running into your fellow doctors in meetings, halls, cafeterias, and office parties. The nurses you have become friendly with will not be around. Your favorite patients will be seeing someone else now. You need to have a plan to replace these interactions in your life, as those people are unlikely to be coming over for dinner.

If you belong to local community organizations, you can get more involved with those—volunteer for more events. If you don't belong to any, now may be the time to join. You might be able to join a hospital committee that includes retired doctors, such as the physician well-being committee or the hospital foundation. You could also establish a routine including morning coffee at your favorite shop and getting to know the other "regulars."

Your work and work environment have been a huge part of your life throughout your professional career. Retirement is a completely new lifestyle, and the more prepared you are to build new relationships and habits to replace those attached to your professional life, the more enjoyment and fulfillment you will find.

Chapter 9

PASSIVE INCOME DURING YOUR RETIREMENT

Most doctors are somewhat familiar with their retirement plans: 401(k), IRA, etc. You are counting on withdrawing that money during your retirement years and using it to live on. This is the first level of passive income available for you during your retirement. But if you are thinking about retiring early, for instance at age 50 or 55, then your retirement plans may not be enough. You may need to look into other sources of passive income you can use to supplement your retirement plan savings.

RESTRICTIONS ON TAX-ADVANTAGED PLANS

The guidelines for tax-advantaged retirement plans use the ages of 59½ as the lower limit of retirement and 70½ on the upper end, for the age at which you can (59½) and must (70½) start withdrawals. Within those boundaries, you are generally able to withdraw any amount you wish from tax-advantaged retirement plans. Withdrawals taken before you are 59½ will generally be penalized. Withdrawals after age 70½ must meet the required minimum distribution, as the government will not let you postpone the taxes forever. If you have a Roth plan, which will not be taxed at withdrawal, you do not have any required minimum distribution.

Not everyone wants to plan their lives around government-chosen age limits. Some of you wish to retire earlier than 59½, while others wish to retire later than 70½. In order for you to have maximum flexibility, you need money stored outside of these government-regulated plans. This additional money will be totally under your control, so you can use it whenever you want. There is one exception to the age-restricted retirement plans: the health savings account (HSA).

THE MOST UNDERRATED, UNDERUTILIZED RETIREMENT PLAN: YOUR HSA

One of the most underrated of the government-regulated savings plans is the health savings account. This is the absolute best of all the retirement plans. You can put the money in pre-tax, it grows tax-free, and you can take it out tax-free as well. There are no age restrictions or required minimum distributions for this account. The only restriction, in order to spend the money tax-free, is the funds must be used for healthcare expenses. If you are over age 65, you can spend the money on anything, but it will be taxed as income, and becomes effectively the same as your 401(k) without the required minimum distribution. It is the best savings vehicle available today.

Just like almost every other government plan, it is not available to everyone. You must meet the qualifications and if you do, you will have a great addition to your overall savings plan. The key component to qualifying is having a high-deductible health insurance plan. These are becoming more and more popular as the cost of healthcare continues to skyrocket. This deductible number changes annually, but for 2017 it must be at least $1,300 for an individual plan or $2,600 for a family plan. If this is the kind of insurance you have, you may qualify for an HSA. As more employers switch to high-deductible health insurance plans, this great savings vehicle will be available to more and more doctors.

Most doctors who have an HSA account do not use it to its fullest advantage.

They tend to spend the money the same year they put it in, thus making their medical expenses pre-tax. Doing this eliminates the long-term tax-free growth possibilities of the account.

A better use of the account is to maximally fund it each year and then not spend any of it until you are actually retired.

In the early years of your professional life, you are younger and usually healthier, and don't have much health expense. During that time, fill your HSA account to the max and pay for your health expenses with either post-tax dollars or through a cafeteria plan at the office, if you have one. (This is a plan that offers employee benefits like covering health-care, orthodontic, and dental care costs, or any other expense the plan agrees to cover for all employees.) Then, when you are older and need more healthcare dollars, your HSA account will be large. If possible, spend the money only on your healthcare needs during retirement. However, if funds are low, you can use it for any other needs in that period and just pay the income taxes on it. This is added retirement savings you can access whenever you want it.

SOURCES OF PASSIVE INCOME

Because of the age restrictions, passive income outside of your retirement accounts is an important factor, if you intend to retire early. This is money available to you at any time, for any need, without any restrictions. Using this source of income means you don't need to take money out of your tax-advantaged accounts, allowing them to continue compounding.

RENTAL PROPERTY

My favorite passive income source is rental property. During the earning years of your life, you can purchase property and use some of your investment money to accelerate the paydown of those property loans. While you are still earning a living from your job, you will not need any of the profits the property is generating, and those profits can also be used to further pay down the loans. Hopefully by the time you retire, all the mortgages on rental property are paid off, or at least much smaller. The lower the debt on the property, the higher the spendable profit your property can generate. This profit is passive income—income not dependent on your individual ability to produce. You earn it even when you are sitting on the beach in Hawaii.

It is important to note the difference between this debt and the debt you have on your personal residence. You should not enter retirement with personal debt, but it is OK to enter retirement with debt on investment property. The distinction is in knowing the difference between an asset and a liability and not using the definition the bank would use—as in, an asset is anything of value. Consider assets as things that put money into your pocket and liabilities as things that take money out of your pocket. The number of liabilities you can own will be limited by your income. Since assets put money into your pocket, you can own an unlimited amount and each new asset

195

will increase your income. Since rental property puts money into your pocket, this debt can be useful. You still want to pay it off as fast as possible, but your own ability to work and earn money is not what is needed to pay this debt.

Just before you retire, consider refinancing all the loans on your rental properties to maximize your cash flow for retirement spending. With the loans being paid down over the years, if you refinance it at this point, you will have a smaller payment, but the rent coming in will not go down and therefore your cash flow will go up.

Let's look at an example. If you own a four-unit apartment complex that had an original loan of $450,000 at 5% interest for 30 years, your payment of principal and interest would have started at $2,415 per month. If each tenant paid $1,200 a month rent, you would take in $4,800 per month. If taxes, insurance, and repairs cost $1,385 a month, you would have a cash flow of $1,000 a month in spendable profit. While you were still working and did not need this profit to live on, you reinvested the $1,000 per month you were making as extra principal payments on the loan. Ten years have now gone by, and you are ready to retire and start living on this profit. After all, you bought this property to help you in your retirement years. If you do not refinance, you will have $1,000 a month of passive income to add to your lifestyle, and you would stop making extra payments on the loan and begin using that cash flow for your retirement income.

During this ten-year period, your extra payments have brought the loan value down to $210,865.

If you were to refinance this loan to start over with the same terms of 30 years at 5% interest, your new payment would be $1,132. Now the income of $4,800 minus the payment of $1,132 and the upkeep costs of $1,385 would leave you with a cash flow of $2,283. The refinance would give you an additional $1,283 a month in spending money, or an extra $15,396 a year. That is quite a hefty increase for simply doing the paperwork of refinancing the loan.

If you have enough of this type of passive income, you will not need to touch your retirement accounts and they will continue to grow tax-free during the early retirement years. Thus, the passive income from your properties will be used to boost your other retirement plan balances for later use. It can also serve as a bridge to age 59½, if you retire early.

Another great advantage afforded by rental property is the depreciation write-off. You can take the value of the property, minus the value of the land, and depreciate that over 27.5 years. In the above example, if your purchase price was $500,000 and the land was worth $100,000, then you could depreciate $400,000, which comes out to $14,545 per year. So the first

$14,545 you make in profit will be tax-free which is close to the additional money you made by refinancing. With the loans paid down and a good portion of the profits being tax-free, income property makes a great supplement to your retirement. Unlike your 401(k), it has no restrictions on how or when you spend the money.

If you were using a property management company or a manager while you were working as a doctor, you could take over that responsibility during your retirement and divert those expenses back into your pocket as well. The additional money you will have from managing your property yourself could allow you to retire several years sooner. If traveling was one of your retirement goals however, you might not want to take over the management responsibilities.

As you can see by this one example, rental property has a great advantage in boosting your retirement income or helping you retire sooner. The cash flow from this one example is $2,283 a month or $27,396 a year, half of it tax-free. Imagine owning ten of them!

START AN INTERNET BUSINESS

The information you have stored away in your head is useful to a lot of people, many of whom would pay for your input. Now might be a good time to consider setting up a blog and teaching your information to the world. The chapter titled Nonclinical Career Alternatives covered this a bit. Now that you are retired, this business could boost your passive income.

You can find lots of advice on the Internet to teach you how to set up your own blog and monetize it. The money coming in from these sources will come in even when you are asleep. If this has been an interest for you, but you were not interested while you were working full time, now would be a good time to start.

OTHER INVESTMENTS

Other ways to generate passive income outside of retirement plans is to buy CDs (certificates of deposit), treasury bills, stocks, bonds, and annuities. Also, a simple savings account or money market account can do this. These are usually very simple for you to acquire and manage, but if even simple investing is not your thing, work with a certified financial planner (CFP) to help you with these.

Selling other assets like your practice, a surgery center, stock in an IPA (Independent Physician Association), share of an office building, or equipment can generate additional income in the early retirement years. Of course, those who are employed will not have some of these things available to sell, which is one of the disadvantages of the employment model.

Whatever you do, it is important for some of your savings and retirement income to be outside of your retirement plans so you have some additional flexibility in the timing of your retirement. Allowing the retirement plan money to continue to grow as long as possible without touching it is an important component to your plan.

I would encourage you to find and play the game Cashflow. This game was developed by Robert Kiyosaki based on the concepts he teaches in his *Rich Dad* series of books. (I don't have any financial connection with him, I just like the game.) The game is similar to Monopoly, but is a lot closer to real life. In order to win the game, you must get out of the rat race (working for a living) by creating passive income that exceeds your expenses. Just like in real life, once your passive income exceeds your expenses, you are financially independent and able to retire. No more need to produce an income by your own working efforts. Debt plays a big factor in the game and every time you pay off a debt, your expenses go down and you are one step closer to exiting the rat race. It makes a great lesson on what it takes to retire and reach the finish line. Play it with your kids and they will learn the perils of debt and the importance of passive income.

USING HOME EQUITY IN RETIREMENT

Another source of money you can use to postpone making withdrawals from your retirement accounts is your home equity. If you are like many doctors and you own a large and expensive house, you can sell it and downsize to a smaller house in your retirement years. Once the kids are gone, your house can be much smaller and still meet all your needs.

Don't overlook your one-time capital gains exemption for your house. The government will allow you to sell your house and downsize once in your life, without capital gains tax on the first $500,000 of gain, if you are married and filing jointly. If your long-term capital gains rate is 15%, you will save $75,000 in taxes by using this exclusion, but only if you know to take it.

DOWNSIZING EXAMPLE

Let's say you own a $1 million house and downsize to a new house valued at $500,000. You will pay no taxes on the swap, one time. Taking closing costs and moving costs into consideration, you may pocket $400,000. Estimated costs of taxes, insurance, utilities, and upkeep run around 3–4% of the value of your house (my house is 3.2%). If you use 3.5% to calculate these expenses, then dropping to the smaller house decreases your annual budget by $17,500.

There are two ways you can use this money from downsizing. First, you could use all of it to live on and postpone the need to make withdrawals from your retirement accounts, allowing them to continue to grow tax-free. For example, if your spending plan requires $100,000 a year for you to live on in your retirement after the $17,500 drop in expenses, the downsize profits would tide you over for four years. A $4 million retirement account growing tax-free for four more years at just 6% interest will increase in value more than $1,000,000 dollars. That is a nice trade for the $400,000 you got from the house.

A second option is to invest the money from downsizing and draw off 4% per year for the rest of your life to supplement the 4% you are taking from your retirement plans. That would be an extra $16,000 a year. If you combine that with the savings in the spending plan from downsizing, then you will increase your available income by $33,500 a year by downsizing.

$$\$16,000 + \$17,500 = \$33,500$$

That extra $33,500 a year could mean the difference between retiring now and having to work a few more years to save enough in the retirement plan to make up for this amount. Since that $33,500 is after taxes, if your retirement plan money will be taxed on withdrawal (assuming 4% annual withdrawal and 25% tax rate in retirement), you would need an additional

$1,122,250 in your retirement plan to stay in the bigger house in retirement. If the money is not taxed (i.e., Roth savings), that total would be $837,500.

$$\$33,500 \times 1.34 \text{ (tax conversion)} \times 25 \text{ (4\% withdrawal)} = \$1,122,250$$

$$\$33,500 \times 25 \text{ (4\% withdrawal)} = \$837,500$$

How long will it take your retirement plan to grow by $1,122,250 or $837,500? That's how much longer you will need to work to stay in the million-dollar house. Looking at it another way, that's how much sooner you can retire if you downsize your house by $500,000. The downsizing equity can play a significant role in your retirement plans and the calculation of your finish line.

If you really want to save time and money in retirement, think about downsizing to a condo. No yard work, minimal upkeep, and when you are traveling, just lock the door and take off. You may find this to be too small a space; I thought I would until I lived in one during my time helping at CAHs and thoroughly enjoyed the lack of responsibility in the smaller space with less stuff. Very freeing. You also don't need to wait for your retirement to downsize and take the savings.

REVERSE MORTGAGES

I mention this option only to condemn it. You should almost never consider using a reverse mortgage. When you see famous people pushing a product on national television, you know the company selling the product is making a lot of profit. If they are making a lot of profit, who do you think is paying them that profit? It is all the people who were convinced to use a reverse mortgage.

A reverse mortgage is basically a home equity line of credit that is extended to you a little at a time. It is offered to those over age 62 who don't think they have enough to live on. The loan will not need to be paid back until you move or die. Then when you die, your heirs will have a mess to clean up in satisfying the terms of the reverse mortgage, especially if they want to keep the house.

First off, they are expensive to get. The upfront fees are often rolled into the loan so you don't notice them, but the bank who charged the fee notices.

You will likely lose the chance to pass on your house to your heirs. By the time you die, there will be a substantial mortgage to pay and the house is likely to be sold to cover it.

If you ever want to move out of the house, to another location or to move into a nursing home, it will likely trigger the sale of your house. Your desire to sell will not be a consideration.

This is a product that should not be considered unless you are running out of money and it is a last-ditch effort to get by. It is a very expensive way to create some cash flow. If your parents used this option and you are stuck with resolving the liability with the bank, it is good to remember the most the bank can take is 95% of the fair market value of the house, regardless of how much they paid the homeowner over the life of the reverse mortgage. So if the house is worth less than the mortgage, don't forget this rule. You could save thousands of dollars knowing this. Don't confuse this with walking away from a house that is under water, where a mortgage you agreed to pay for purchasing a house is larger than the current market value of the house. That is different and unethical, since you agreed to repay that amount of money. With the reverse mortgage, the bank is taking a risk that the payments they make to you will not catch up to the value of the house. If you live a long time, they will lose on their bet. To their benefit, their bet will likely be covered by the FHA insurance they have.

Before you or your parents consider a reverse mortgage, look at other options:

- ✓ Sell your house and purchase a less expensive one and live on the equity.
- ✓ Sell your house and rent a smaller one and live on the equity.
- ✓ Sell your house and buy an RV to live in.

✓ Sell your house and move in with the kids.

✓ Sell your house and house-sit for missionaries.

✓ Sell your house and live in your kid's guest house.

Look closely at developing passive income sources and at other sources of income you can access as part of your retirement planning, especially if you plan to retire early, before age 59½.

Chapter 10

LIFESTYLE CHANGES IN RETIREMENT

Retirement should be exciting. All the things you have wanted to do but couldn't find the time to do when you were working, you will now have time to do. Or so you think. I've said for years that working gets in the way of all the stuff I want to do. When the job ends, the void it leaves will fill up fast, and if you are not careful, it will be full before you even get to the things you wanted to do. Many doctors are type A personalities and don't like having nothing to do, so don't be surprised when your schedule fills right up.

Speaking of schedules, be sure you make one for your new life. If you just stop working and don't create some structure, you may feel like you are just drifting and not like the feeling. Your life has been very scheduled up until now and throwing that structure out can be a bit disorienting. Plan for a successful retirement the same way you planned for a successful career.

I thought I would be able to catch up on everything around the house when I stopped working full time. My desires and my reality did not match. Now, three years after cleaning out my office and moving everything into the garage, it still sits, and I haven't had the time to deal with it and put everything where it should go. So I discovered even in semi-retirement, this is still true:

The state of "caught up" doesn't exist.

Before you actually retire and start all these projects you have been dying to do, I suggest you make a list of them. It would be a good time to write out a "bucket list," everything you would like to do and experience before you leave this earth. Put everything in some sort of priority order so you will be sure to accomplish the important ones and not have the great stuff covered over by the good stuff. Yes, your to-do list will still exist after you retire. If you establish some priorities beforehand, you will be much more likely to have your retirement be all you imagined.

FIRST, TAKE A VACATION

I suggest the first thing you do when you retire is go on a vacation. This is a transition period in your life, so make a clean break. Go somewhere new or to a favorite getaway and decompress, and don't worry about how long it will last. Enjoy yourself, knowing you won't have any office paperwork to catch up on when you return. When you do get home, it will be to start your new life as a retired doctor.

Many doctors have not done much vacationing during their careers. A friend of mine began to ease into retirement by cutting back his practice to half time, two weeks on and two weeks off. He vacationed with his wife that first two weeks and came home with the realization he had never taken fourteen days off in a row at any point in his career. He really liked that vacation and for the first time realized what he had missed during his working years by not giving himself more time to relax. The first week was all about decompressing and the second week he was truly relaxed. If this describes you as well, make your first vacation getaway fairly short, two to three weeks, or you may find yourself feeling like a fish out of water. Ease into all this leisure time.

Plan this first vacation carefully so that it will meet your needs. What are your vacation objectives? Do you need some decompression time? If so, plan a vacation that will be restful, like a couple of weeks on the beach with no planned activities. Read a book for fun, visit a nearby museum, see a play, take in a ballgame, and look forward to eating out at a nice restaurant. Do you want to explore some things you have had on your bucket list for far too long? Then pick an easy one to be the first out of the gate. Don't try to do everything at once. You will be retired for a long time, so spread your bucket list out and don't try to do everything in the first six months. It is a marathon, not a sprint.

A NEW HOUSE

Many retirees want to move to a new location for their retirement or downsize their house. Some want to get out of the cold in Chicago and move to Arizona. Some want to get out of the heat in Arizona and move to Oregon. Some want to move closer to their children, grandchildren, or parents. Whatever move you want to make, don't plan on doing it right away.

As good as you think it might be, adjusting to retirement can be a major life stressor. Moving is another major life stressor. It is not good to pile them on top of each other. Take on one stress at a time. Get settled into the routine of being retired before you change everything by moving to a new location. Get used to being with your spouse more. Get over the loss you will feel from not going to work every day. As much as you are ready to stop, it will leave a hole in your life. After all, work has been the bulk of your daily schedule for many years. It will take a while to get used to being retired.

After the initial stress of retirement fades, then you can begin your search for a new home in the area you want to move to.

Maybe try it out for a while first. If you are thinking of moving to Arizona, rent a house there for a couple of months to see what it is like. Try it for more than one season. As I described in my book *The Doctors Guide to Starting Your Practice Right*, renting when you move to a new area could save you a lot of money. Buying and selling a house is expensive, and it takes about five years (on average) before market appreciation will recover the closing costs. If you move to Arizona, buy a house, and one year later decide you don't like the weather as well as you anticipated, you are likely to lose money on the house when you sell. If you rent in the area for that year and you have that revelation, you can easily walk away and rent something in the next area. You can keep renting in different places until you find what you are looking for. Even moving to be near your kids might not turn out as you thought. Renting enables you to keep your options open with less financial risk.

Don't underestimate the effect of losing all your usual support when you move. You will need to make new friends, find a new place of worship, establish care with a new doctor, find a barber/hairdresser, and find a new dentist. Groups you belonged to like Rotary Club, the Masonic lodge, book clubs, and bridge clubs will need to be replaced. You will have to learn the new town so you know where to buy goods and any special items you have grown to like, such as particular spices or hobby supplies. Losing all the things you were familiar with might be worse than the joy of the new location.

A SECOND HOME

Many retired doctors want to have a second home; in fact, they purchase it before retiring, so the outlay happened while they were still earning money. It can be nice to live in Florida in the winter and Minnesota in the summer. Just understand this will be more expensive than you think.

You will have the costs and upkeep of two homes. You will also have the costs of traveling between homes. You will need to make arrangements for them to be empty for extended periods of time. Empty homes can have deterioration problems. For example, if there is a water leak, no one is there to find it and additional damage can occur.

We had something like that happen to us. We were away for an extended time and my son was checking on our house now and then. One day he went in to find it was very humid and there was a gurgling noise coming from the heater vents. When he looked in one of them, he saw it was full of water. A recent heavy rainstorm had caused a ditch behind our house to spill over and it flooded the crawl space under our house, filling the heating ducts with water. Had he not checked on the house, we might have had a severe mold problem and a destroyed heating system. Luckily for us, he caught it early enough and was able to pump out the crawlspace and dry it without any damage.

You will save a lot of money if you rent your second home rather than buy. You can go to a different place each year and experience something new. Then you only have one empty house to be concerned about. The rental will be much cheaper than owning a second house. You will have a little more trouble and effort moving your things, but most places where you would desire to spend the winter will have furnished houses for rent.

TRAVEL

This is on the immediate agenda for many retirees. They have been tied down to their job for so long and now that they are free, they want to spread their wings and fly all over the world. Travel is expensive, and you need to make arrangements for this in your retirement spending plan if you want it to be successful. Travel expenses range widely, depending on how and in what style you want to do it. RVing around the country has a big startup cost and then the ongoing cost is fairly low, but may be more than you anticipate.

When you are creating your spending plan, figure out whether you want to go on high-end trips or less expensive package deals, which come in a wide range too. This makes a huge difference. As I began searching travel options, I found some wild and crazy things. I got one brochure for a guided private jet tour around the world for 25 days that would cost us only $230,000. The price had an asterisk though. If we were not a member of the organization, it would be an extra $300 each.

On a more reasonable note, we took a one-month tour of France and Italy in 2013 that included two weeks guided, one week traveling on our own, and one week in a timeshare for $14,500. That's less than 7% of the cost of the expensive trip, which I'm sure would not have been sixteen times better. You can make some fabulous travel arrangements for not very much money. And don't forget, before you go jetting off to Europe, there are some great places in the United States you probably haven't been to yet, and they don't require a passport.

One thing to keep in mind as you begin to travel is how to handle what you leave behind. Someone will need to care for your yard, check on your house, and water your houseplants. If you have pets, arrangements will need to be made if they don't travel with you. The mail will need to be dealt with somehow; stopping and starting the mail with each trip can become a pain. You might consider a giant locking mailbox with a capacity for one month's worth of mail. Then you won't need to do anything about the mail when you leave. When you get home, the mail is all there. Even if you return at 8:00 p.m., you don't have to wait for the post office to open before getting the mail. Then there is the newspaper—you do not want papers piling up on your doorstep, announcing to the world you are not home. Best to stop delivery for the time you are gone.

CRUISE SHIPS

An interesting option not available to you while you are working is to live on a cruise ship. This can even serve as an alternative to assisted living. You move into a room on the ship and just go where it goes. The price will be discounted for multiple bookings, back to back. You will get free food, live entertainment, transportation throughout the world, movies, room service, maid service, daily bed turndown with a chocolate, fresh sheets and towels, dancing lessons, evenings out for dancing, games, lectures, puzzles, books, gym membership, swimming pools, hot tubs, group activities, new people to meet weekly, church services, parties, medical care, art shows, cooking classes, and so much more.

You probably haven't considered this one before. The cost of all the things you get on a cruise ship may even be cheaper than living in your current house. The full price for an inside cabin on one ten-day Caribbean cruise I just looked up is $899. You and your spouse for a month is $5,394 before any multiple cruise discounts. That is $65,000 a year for all the services I listed above for two people. That is a pretty good lifestyle in retirement for a pretty reasonable cost.

HOBBIES

You may have a nice hobby you would like to expand. If you are a musician, you might consider putting together a band. You might expand your woodworking skills. Or even take the time to finally write that book floating around in your head all these years. Be sure you make time for your hobbies as you contemplate your new schedule in retirement.

During your career, you probably didn't have as much time to devote to your hobbies as you wanted. Now you can spend as much time on them as you want. Do you have everything you need? Do you need some fresh new tools? A new instrument? A motorhome? Some hiking gear? A new camera?

Whatever you have in mind, you should have both the time and the money to make it great. This could be the time to golf every Jack Nicklaus course in the country. Or camp in every national park, or take a photograph of every bird in America, or ride Route 66. Go for it and have a ball. Just keep an eye on the spending so it doesn't get out of hand. It doesn't have to cost a mint to have fun.

FRIENDS AND RELATIVES

Now is a great time to visit friends and relatives. However, be sure they want you to visit, and don't overstay your welcome, especially if they aren't retired yet. Maybe the kids have moved away and you would like to visit your grandkids. What will you do for sleeping? Live in their house? Nearby hotel? Park your RV in their driveway? Each of these has advantages and disadvantages to think about before you embark.

You can kill two birds with one stone by traveling with friends and relatives. When you are retired and have the money to travel a lot, be considerate of your friends and relatives who do not have such a luxury and spread it around a bit. Go with different people on each trip. For example, take a trip to Florida with your spouse, then a Mediterranean cruise with a group of friends, then a cruise to Alaska with your kids, then a paddleboat cruise up the Columbia River with your parents, and then top it off with a trip to Hawaii as a couple. You can combine your traveling and spending time with friends and relatives into one activity. Traveling with friends is a lot of fun. Just be sure you schedule some time together and some time apart, otherwise you might wear out your welcome with each other.

Many retirees pull babysitting duty with the grandkids. Your children enjoy the break for some R&R together, and you enjoy time with your grandchildren. It's a win-win deal. You may even decide to move closer to them to increase these benefits. But think carefully before agreeing to be the daily daycare provider for your grandchildren. Such a commitment could make it impossible to do the things you always dreamed you would do in retirement.

Think carefully about lifestyle changes before taking new steps. How will you use your time? How will you pay for the new stuff? Will you buy it before or after you stop working? How will your spouse adjust to you being home all the time? Will you spend more time with your children or grandchildren? Are there other family members you might want to be closer to? Will your parents need your help?

DON'T LOSE YOUR HEALTH

Don't forget about getting enough sleep and exercise. You tend to forget these important aspects as you begin to play more. Just because you don't have to get up in the morning doesn't mean you can stay up late. Keep a reasonable schedule to keep some structure in your life. You will enjoy your life during your retirement years if you take good care of yourself. You want to stay strong so you can carry your suitcase through the airport (even if it does have wheels).

Older people especially need to work on strength training. As we age, so do our muscles, and atrophy and subsequent weakness can become a problem. We also tend to be less active after retiring. Older people do not go out and play a little basketball or soccer in the afternoon like their kids or grandkids do. Make it a point to either have strength training equipment at home or go to a gym regularly, at least three to four times a week. A problem area to consider is having sufficient strength in your glutes and quads to easily get in and out of a chair. Be sure squats or stair climbing are in your weekly exercise routine, or one day you will not be able to get up if you fall.

When my wife and I decided to take my grandmother, who was in her 80s and recovering from a stroke, on a road trip to the International Peace Gardens, we put her on a pre-vacation exercise routine. She made incredible improvements in her leg strength in a very short time. She needed to be able to walk a lot and negotiate the five steps into our motorhome. I was surprised at how quickly her abilities changed by simply adopting an exercise routine.

One of the changes we made in my grandmother's routine was to add stair climbing. She liked to go to the mall and walk. It was indoors and climate controlled so she could do it in any weather. We modified her routine a bit to include walking up and down the stairs at each end of the mall. Within a month she was able to climb the stairs into our motorhome without assistance. Before she added stairs, she needed a lot of help to get into our motorhome.

She also had a problem with her shoulder and had lost significant range of motion. This had been a problem for years. In the three weeks she was in the motorhome, she had to walk her fingers up the wall every time she passed by the bathroom on the way to her room in the back. Within one week she had regained full range of motion in her shoulder. Doing the exercises regularly and often made all the difference. With better joint range of motion and leg strength, she had a much better time on her travels. Best advice: Don't let yourself deteriorate in the first place, stay active, and make exercise a normal part of your routine.

RETIREMENT IS A WHOLE NEW WAY OF LIFE

Retirement is a whole new way of life, and a great time to test out new living locations and other options. Don't commit to what you thought was your dream too quickly. Allow yourself the chance to make sure it's what you want before you buy a house in the wrong place or a second house you end up not using. Think about what is really important to you and prioritize those things to do first. With a little planning, you will have a wonderful life in retirement.

Chapter 11

BEYOND THE FINISH LINE AND ESTATE ISSUES

If you avoided paying years of interest by getting out of debt and socked away a good portion of your money from the start, you should have more than enough money to live on for the rest of your life. Maybe you even set your finish line too high and didn't realize it until after you had been living on your retirement funds for a while. You will likely have a significant inheritance to pass on to your family. You—or more accurately, your heirs—may even be faced with a significant estate tax if you don't do everything right.

PASSING ON YOUR ESTATE

Consider getting the advice of an estate-planning attorney. You may benefit from creating a trust if you don't already have one. If you do have one, you should look into any needed revisions. If you initially set up your living trust when your children were young and now they are young adults, your trust is unlikely to still represent what you want to happen to your estate.

When your estate includes grandchildren, considerations become more complex. What will happen in the case where your two children die before you do and one of them has one child and the other has three? Do you want all four grandchildren to divide up your estate evenly, or would the only child get half and the other three split the other half, as would have happened if your children were still alive? If you don't spell this out, there will be a fight for your money. The proceeds for the only child swing from 50% of your estate to 25% in these two scenarios. If that is a swing of a million dollars, you can count on some strife. Make sure your wishes are clear.

Another thing an attorney can do is help you minimize estate taxes. There are legitimate ways to avoid this expensive tax. The government would prefer you to put your money to good use rather than stockpile it, so they have built in incentives to do so. Understanding the rules can make a huge difference in your estate taxes. It will especially come into play as your estate passes the $5.49 million mark, the threshold for federal estate taxes in 2017.

Unfortunately, the limits on paying estate tax is a moving target. For a married couple in 2003, it was a million dollars; it has increased to $5.49 million per spouse for 2017. If you don't do it right, a couple can only give $5.49 million to their heirs tax-free. If you play the game well, you can double that. Keeping that extra $5.49 million in play without paying the 40% federal tax will save your heirs almost $2.2 million in taxes. If your estate is less than the $5.49 million exclusion, then federal taxes will not be a concern—until Congress changes the rules again.

The issue of losing this exclusion comes when the first person of a married couple dies.

Normally when the first spouse dies, their portion of the estate goes to the remaining living spouse, which is tax-free. Then when the second spouse dies, the heirs will get the remaining estate. Since only one heir is passing on money at that time, only one of the $5.49 million exclusions applies. The other was lost when the first to die did not use it to pass money on to their heirs rather than their spouse.

To save this exclusion, the first to die must pass on their share of the money to someone other than their spouse. In most cases this is not desirable, as the remaining spouse may still need it. This is where a trust can come in handy.

You can set up a trust to contain all of the family assets. When the first spouse dies, the amount of the assets matching the inheritance exclusion could be passed on to your children in the form of a new trust the remaining spouse will control. The remaining spouse can use the money in this new trust while he or she is still alive as needed. Upon the second spouse's death, this trust will then be controlled by the heirs, and any appreciation of that trust is not part of the estate. Then the second spouse will be able to pass on an additional $5.49 million, federal tax-free. I know it sounds complicated and that's why an estate attorney will be needed to set it all up.

PHILANTHROPY

You may want to limit what you pass on to your heirs to this figure and then they will not be paying federal estate taxes. In order to do this, you will need to give away money to keep under this threshold. Eleven million dollars is a good inheritance; more is not going to really help your heirs.

If you do have such a large estate, your retirement needs should be taken care of just fine. Most doctors will never reach this level of wealth, but some will. If you do, you can make some incredible gifts while you are still alive to see them work. Here is a good chance to support those things that are important to you. Your money can help religious groups, social groups, political groups, the arts, or community projects you feel are important. I am reminded of a quote I heard from Larry Burkett, as he was talking about a wealthy friend of his he didn't name. His friend had a saying:

I do my givin' while I'm livin' so I'm knowin' where it's goin'.

Any one person can currently (2017) give $14,000 to any other person without paying a gift tax. This number also changes every year. The reason for the gift tax is to keep people from avoiding income or estate taxes. For example, without a gift tax, you could hire your daughter to work for your company and only pay her $1 a year. You would then give her $100,000 a year and she would not pay any income or inheritance tax on the money. The government stopped that from happening by limiting the amount you can give. In that example, if you wanted her to get $100,000 while working in your office, you could give her $14,000 and your spouse could give her $14,000, and then you could pay her the other $72,000 in salary, which would be taxable. Or, you could take it even further and each spouse give your daughter's spouse $14,000 as well and pay her the remaining $44,000 as earned income.

Giving away portions of a large estate while you are still alive can be very rewarding. Why wait until you are gone for them to get the money? If you are not going to need it and they can use it, why not give it now and enjoy seeing how it is used?

If you had two children and four grandchildren, you and your spouse each could give each of them $14,000. That would be $28,000 to each of the six individuals for a total estate shrinkage without taxes of $168,000 a year. If you feel they should not have access to the money at this time, as in the four-year-old granddaughter is not ready to handle $28,000, you can put it into a trust. That trust can be responsible for paying for your grandchildren's college expenses, and they may get a college education without amassing any debt.

There are other fancy ways to handle your retirement funds, such as passing on an IRA to a grandchild instead of a child to increase the length of time it can grow tax-free. Having a good estate attorney to help you with these details will be of great benefit, especially since the rules change from time to time.

HOW TO INCREASE YOUR DONATIONS TO CHARITY WITHOUT REALLY TRYING

Maybe you feel strongly about supporting a charitable organization. They could probably use the money now instead of after you die. You can give them any amount and the gift won't be taxed. You may be able to use the write-off for the charitable gift to offset the taxes you will owe for your required minimum distribution from your retirement plan.

There is great reward in seeing your hard-earned money put to good use. Think about where you would like to make a difference. Don't let a big stockpile of money just sit there and wait for you to die.

When deciding how you will give, consider giving appreciated assets instead of cash. For example, suppose you bought a building for $200,000 that is now worth $2 million. If you sell the building, you will pay taxes on the $1.8 million profit and then can give the rest to your charity. If you gave them the building instead, they can sell it for $2 million and no tax will be owed. If you owned the property for more than a year, you also get the fair market value as a deduction on your tax return. So giving them the building and letting them sell it puts both you and the charity money ahead.

When you control the money, you can be sure it goes where you want it to go. After you are gone, you will not get to enjoy seeing what happens, and you will not have the same control in a will or trust as you do when you are still alive.

WILLS AND TRUSTS

This is a good time to be sure your will and your trust, if you have one, are up to date and in good order. If you don't have a will, get one made this month. Don't finish reading this chapter without making an appointment with an attorney to draw up your will. You do not want the court deciding what happens to your estate. The musician Prince died suddenly without a will, and it caused a lot of bickering between distant relatives who fought over control of his money. He probably has a bigger estate to fight over than you will have, but whatever size your estate is, do you really want your family to fight over it?

Wills and trusts should be updated about every five years. Things change in your life, and you don't want your sudden unexpected demise to cause trouble if you haven't updated for those changes. Fighting occurs even over small estates. To some people, what happens to a $30,000 estate is important enough to cause a family feud. So your estate, which will likely be much larger, may create some bickering if you don't have it all laid out. Even the best of wills or trusts might get contested, but you should do everything you can to be sure your estate will be handled the way you want it to be handled. Schedule a meeting with your heirs to tell them ahead of time how you plan to handle the passing on of your estate. The more planning you do, the smoother the transition will be when you are gone.

ADVANCE DIRECTIVES

Don't forget to have your advance directives in place. This includes your durable power of attorney for healthcare (DPOAHC), living will, and in some states a MOLST (Medical Orders for Life Sustaining Treatment) or POLST (Physician Orders for Life Sustaining Treatment) form. The most important of these is your DPOAHC which defines who will make healthcare decisions for you if you are no longer able to do so for yourself. It is best to appoint a second and even third choice just in case your first choice is unable to be reached or is unable to serve in this capacity. The DPOAHC is who your doctor will look to for decisions on life support and other important healthcare choices, if you are unable to make these decisions yourself. Be sure those you choose are willing to fill this role *and* that they know your wishes.

If you have these directives completed and you have had a sit-down talk with your spouse and children about your wishes, you will be taking a great burden from them. Your family will have much more peace about deciding to end life support if they know it was your wish to do so and not their decision totally. Watching my parents go through this with the deaths and disabilities of my grandmothers gave me a great appreciation for how much burden my grandmothers had removed from my parents during that difficult time by communicating their wishes. My parents knew exactly what their parents wanted, so it was a little less stressful for them during those final days. Do your family a favor and sit down for this talk.

Also, don't make them have to decide where you will be buried or if you should be cremated. They will be dealing with the grief of your death, so don't add more to their plate during that trying time. If you decide to preplan and pay for your funeral and burial expenses, be sure the information and receipts are readily available to your heirs. If they don't know about it, they will likely pay for these services a second time. The funeral home is not responsible for keeping these receipts; you are.

A general power of attorney (not for healthcare, which is separate) is also important to have in place. If you are still alive but incapacitated and not able to make decisions, you will have the mechanism in place for your family to take care of your estate for you. They will be able to pay your bills and handle the little things that come up. You will be surprised how difficult it will be for you to cancel a cell phone contract if you are not the person who opened it or the person with the power of attorney. Fort Knox should be so secure.

TAKE CARE OF THE DETAILS SO YOU CAN TRULY RELAX

In summary, crossing the finish line knowing you have all your ducks in a row is very satisfying. Take as much of the worry out of your life as you can and enjoy your retirement years. Don't blow your money on frivolous things like a different car for every day of the week simply because you can. Put your money to good use and enjoy the rest of the journey that is your life.

QUESTIONS? COMMENTS?

Dr. Cory S. Fawcett
FinancialSuccessMD.com

I wrote this book to share what I have learned so your life can be better and you can enjoy the benefits of being a doctor. I also want to hear about your experiences. Any feedback is welcome, and I want to know if you think I've missed an important topic, or you have a story to tell or found a mistake. Also, I didn't put everything I know into this book. Send me an email at md@financialsuccessmd.com or contact me through my website at FinancialSuccessMD.com.

If you found this book to be useful, please post a review on Amazon, spread the word in social media, and pass on what you have learned to your colleagues.

Connect with Financial Success MD on LinkedIn
Like @FinancialSuccessMD on Facebook
Follow @Fin_SuccessMD on Twitter
Email md@financialsuccessmd.com
Watch Financial Success MD on YouTube
Follow my blog at FinancialSuccessMD.com
Join me at financialsuccessmd on Instagram
Pin me at financialsuccessmd on Pinterest

Acknowledgments

Many people contributed to the knowledge contained in this book, but I need to give a special thanks to Steven Babitsky, Esq., and James J. Mangraviti Jr., Esq., who introduced me to the concept of nonclinical careers for physicians. Curiosity led me to attend their SEAK, Inc. conference in 2014 and discovered a whole new world of possibilities for doctors who are struggling with their careers. That conference birthed my consulting business, Prescription for Financial Success, and my *The Doctors Guide* book series. This book was written to help all the hurting doctors who are ready to quit practicing medicine. It also provides the tools you will need to prepare for that day when you will take down your shingle for good. I hope I can spark an idea that will either rejuvenate your current practice or give you a fresh new direction to go with your knowledge and experience.

A special thanks to those who did the test reading of this book and offered suggested improvement: R. J. Leavitt, MD; Allison Batchelor, MD, CMD; Helane Fronek, MD, FACP; James Haeberlin, MD, FACS; Michelle Mudge-Riley, DO, MHA, RD, LD, CLT; Pamela Wible, MD; Kernan Manion, MD; Karl Ordelheide, MD; Nathan Kemalyan, MD, FACS; and my lovely wife, Carolyn Fawcett.

Also those who contributed their story of success in seeking a clinical or nonclinical alternative to spice up or extend their careers: David Appleby, MD; Mark Deatherage, MD, FACS; Pamela Wible, MD; A.J., MD; Kevin Pho, MD; Michelle Mudge-Riley, DO, MHA, RD, LD, CLT; James M. Dahle, MD.

There are many others along the way who contributed to the information I've learned during my career and am now passing on to you. I'm sorry I can't list them all, or even remember them all, as they are too numerous to count.

Thanks to the team at Aloha Publishing, including Maryanna Young and Jennifer Regner, and the Fusion Creative Works design team of Shiloh Schroeder, Rachel Langaker, and Jessi Carpenter. Without them, this book would still be just an idea floating around in my mind.

About the Author

Dr. Cory S. Fawcett's passion for teaching personal finance spans his entire career. Through one-on-one counseling, as a Crown Financial Ministries small group discussion leader (a ten-week Bible study on money management), and as a keynote speaker, he has been improving people's financial and professional lives for years. As an instructor for medical students and residents, he has found they have a hunger and need for financial wisdom and direction as they transform into practicing physicians. He is the author of *The Doctors Guide* book series, including the award-winning *The Doctors Guide to Starting Your Practice Right* and *The Doctors Guide to Eliminating Debt.*

With his financial interest and background knowledge, he has served on several boards and financial committees throughout the years. He has been involved as owner, founder, or partner in more than two dozen business and real estate ventures.

The lack of surgeons in rural areas and his desire to work less led him to the decision to leave his twenty-year practice, in a town with ten general surgeons, and assist in underserved areas. In February 2014 he began a three-year journey of working part time in rural Pacific Northwest towns with only one or two surgeons. With just one surgeon in town, the call burden of 24/7 availability is unsustainable. Dr. Fawcett provided them with a needed break from their pager, helping to keep these rural surgeons healthy. This plan also allowed for him to extend his practice another three years while working at a slower pace.

His current mission is teaching doctors to have healthy, happy, and debt-free lives—to regain control of their practice, their time, and their finances. He is writing, speaking, and coaching in an effort to improve the lives of his colleagues. Burnout, suicide, debt, and bankruptcy are increasing among physicians, dentists, optometrists, chiropractors, pharmacists, nurse practitioners, and others in the healthcare industry, and he focuses on halting the progression of these unnecessary outcomes.

Dr. Fawcett is an award-winning author, keynote speaker, entrepreneur, and a repurposed general surgeon. He completed his bachelor's degree in biology at Stanford University, his doctor of medicine at Oregon Health Sciences University, and his general surgery residency at Kern Medical Center. After completing his training, he returned to southern Oregon to practice for twenty years in a single specialty, private practice group in Grants Pass. Then for three years, he worked part time in rural hospitals providing call coverage before devoting his time to helping healthcare professionals thrive. Since 1988 he has shared his home with his lovely bride, Carolyn. They have two boys: Brian, who graduated from college with a degree in economics, and Keith, who is currently working on a degree in mobile development.

Made in the USA
Monee, IL
24 June 2021

72230784R00134